NORTHERN TERRITORY

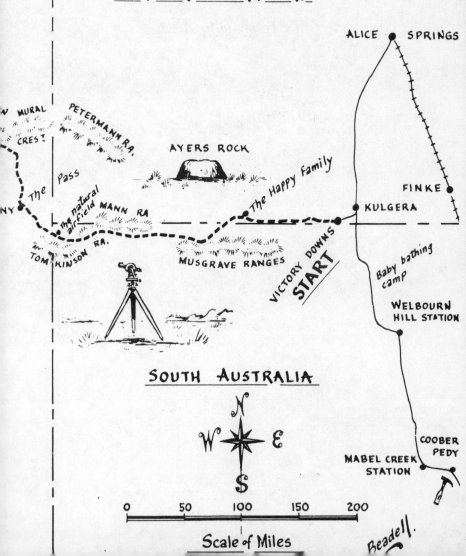

N MURAL CREST

PETERMANN RA.

AYERS ROCK

The Pass

the natural airfield MANN RA.

NY

TOM KINSON RA.

MUSGRAVE RANGES

The Happy Family

ALICE SPRINGS

FINKE

KULGERA

Baby bathing camp

VICTORY DOWNS **START**

WELBOURN HILL STATION

COOBER PEDY

MABEL CREEK STATION

SOUTH AUSTRALIA

W   N   E
    S

0	50	100	150	200

Scale of Miles

Beadell.

To my wife, Anne

LEN BEADELL

TOO LONG IN THE BUSH

LANSDOWNE

Books by Len Beadell:

Too Long in the Bush
Blast the Bush
Bush Bashers
Still in the Bush
Beating About the Bush
Outback Highways (a selection)
End of an Era

Published by Lansdowne Publishing Pty Ltd
Level 1, Argyle Centre,
18 Argyle Street, Sydney NSW 2000, Australia

First published 1965
Reprinted 1966 (twice), 1967, 1969, 1970, 1971, 1972, 1974,
1975, 1976, 1980
Limp edition 1985
Reprinted 1989
Reprinted by Lansdowne Publishing Pty Ltd 1994, 1997, 1998

Wholly designed and typeset in Australia
Printed in Australia by McPherson's Printing Group

National Library of Australia Cataloguing-in-Publication Data

Beadell, Len, 1923–
   Too long in the bush.

   ISBN 1 86302 404 9.

   1. Roads—Australia, Central—Design and construction.
   2. Australia, Central—Description and travel. 3. Gunbarrel
   Highway (W.A.). I. Title.

625.709942

Contents

Illustrations

Introduction

Everyone knows the world is round. Most people believe that it is spherical and many have heard that it is a little flattened at the top and bottom. But there are a few people whose job it is to try to discover more about the problems the earth's shape presents, and their study is known as "geodesy."

This knowlege of the world's dimensions is needed, with ever increasing accuracy, to help in the development of such projects as space rockets and guided missiles. It is not so long ago that a good average figure of the earth was enough for map making and navigation, but that is not enough today.

A series of measurements under the name of a geodetic survey must be taken over large portions of the earth's surface before geodesists can begin work on their calculations, and these surveys are made with almost complete disregard for the nature of the terrain. Mountains offering near impossible resistance, burning deserts, and disease-infested jungles have been, and are still being, attacked the world over — such is the important need for geodetic surveys. Information obtained from them is pooled, and it all helps towards giving us an overall picture. The measurements take the form of a great number of points fixed in relationship to each other by instruments with the greatest precision possible, and they follow the course on the ground in the direction of the currently required geodetic link on paper.

Many such long-needed links have never been made, simply because the areas, up to the present time, have defied penetration. Greater effort has recently been put into the onslaught of some of these with the arrival of new-type instruments, vehicles, and air support, and, in some cases, of heavy equipment for the carving of access roads in advance. One such area lies to the west of the centre of

Australia and comprises almost a thousand miles of desolate, waterless semi-desert, uninhabited except for the few small tribes of aborigines.

The story of the making of the first access road through the middle of this region, for the initial purpose of a geodetic link, is told in *Too Long in the Bush*, an outback phrase applied to anybody who, after being in remote places for lengthy periods, appears to the Town Dweller to be just a trifle *different* . . .

1

The Happy Family

Even if the sun is too hot, people don't usually ask you to drive your vehicle into their lounge-room unless they know you. At least, not without saying hello first. But after seeing the heavy motor bike leaning against the wardrobe, it didn't seem so very unusual when this happened to me.

A man was sitting on a bed covered with tools, working on a truck, and a girl of about fifteen sat on a bullock-hide chair playing a guitar. A white-haired woman swayed back and forth on a rocking-chair, knitting. This could be seen at a glance, as the house had no walls and the floor was the same as the surrounding desert, except for the spinifex. This had been scraped off and heaped on the wire netting roof, which was held up by a series of black oak posts with stock-whips and bridles hanging from nails in them. Before I could switch off the engine of my Land-Rover, another woman, who had been attending to a baby in a box on a petrol drum in the sitting room, hurried over to the set of sliprails between the road and the house. Pulling the sliprails back she beckoned to me to come in out of the sun, Land-Rover and all. After steering carefully past a chest of drawers, I stopped short of a kerosene refrigerator. Before I could give any indication as to who I was, or the reason for and possible duration of my visit, they told me where my place was to be at the table and where I would be sleeping.

I had really only just dropped in after completing a reconnaissance survey for the first hundred miles of my new project — a road access across the geographical centre of Australia, from the Alice Springs road near the South Australian border to Carnegie cattle station nine hundred miles away to the west.

Before I had time to explain, a girl of about eighteen with a branding iron in her hand appeared from behind the stove, and announced that they now had one black snake fewer for grandma to frighten away when she went to bed. Grandma smiled from her rocking-chair. She apparently slept in the screened-off section of the house done out in hessian. She told me she often found snakes coiled up on her bed in the cool, but it was quite all right as they went away when she rattled a treacle tin full of stones that she kept especially for this purpose. Her bed was made of flour bags stretched between log rails.

The man working on the truck in the bedroom must have decided he'd done enough mechanical work for a while, and he dropped the grease gun on his bed. I was about to tell him I came from the Rocket Range, and that he would soon be seeing some activity around his station, when he asked in a loud voice who was game enough to go for a ride with him on his motor bike. The guitar and branding iron were immediately discarded, and Miss Guitar, leaving the pillion seat to Miss Branding Iron, took her usual place on the headlight. The man had the machine revved to full throttle and took off with a cowboy's "Yippeee!" travelling at twenty miles an hour before he had passed the sink. They were doing thirty-five as they roared passed the dressing table, with their hats, held by thongs around their necks, flying behind. After they had disappeared from sight over a sand ridge alongside the house, Grandma merely looked up and said, "Noisy things, ain't they?"

It seemed as if I'd lived there for years, the way this family carried on. Paying me no attention at all, they made me feel more welcome than if they had laid out a red carpet.

The lady of the sliprails handed me a curved skinning knife and, pointed to a shade house, said we wanted some steak for dinner, and I'd find a bullock's leg hanging there. It was almost midday. Everyone is expected to be able to do anything in the bush, the theory being that if you don't

know how, right now is the best time to learn. As I came back with the meat, it struck me that no one had even said "Hello" yet but it didn't seem necessary.

The motor bike, coming in from the opposite direction, careered through the house without the slightest hesitation. As it raced past Grandma, who was sitting forward in her rocking-chair, knitting, I noticed the offside handlebar hook in her wool. When the dust cleared she was smiling, holding the two empty knitting needles, as a single strand of wool travelled at forty miles an hour over the sandhill. She simply said, "Fast, ain't they? Now what was I knitting?"

On the next circuit the riders were flagged down with a tea towel, and the simmering motor bike was returned to the wardrobe.

Bush people are always glad to see strangers, and they take it for granted you're okay or you wouldn't be out there in the first place. So during dinner I wasn't surprised when they asked casually how many weeks I would be staying with them. I could now, at last, tell them I was from Woomera, and what I was doing here. On hearing of my road project, the man asked if I was the feller he'd heard tell about, making a few new roads hereabouts, and did I have a bulldozer? He could sure use a turkey's nest dam by the mill.

I told him we did have a bulldozer, and a grader too, with a small party of five men, three trucks, and my Land-Rover. I asked if they would sell us beef from time to time, because theirs was the last homestead we'd be seeing for the entire distance. We planned to establish a new weather recording station half-way over at the Rawlinson Ranges, and for this a construction party would soon be along who would be glad of any meat and water these people could let them have.

Their curiosity mounted as to the purpose of this new road, and I explained that an Australia-wide survey was under way for measuring the earth's surface; this was needed to help any large-scale project for development. When the area came anywhere near the country covered by our testing range, we gave all our assistance with access roads and a reconnaissance of the hundreds of thousands of square miles involved. Next would come the trig survey, as we called it, resulting in accurate maps. As this country was mostly unexplored, apart from an occasional expedition in the 1800s, the place was as yet unmapped.

When I told them how I would find my way, they seemed somewhat doubtful. They pointed out that it wouldn't be much good looking at the stars, because they kept moving all the time.

The Happy Family were, by now, firing questions, getting more excited at the prospect of all this activity, and planning with a gleam in their eye how the new road would help them muster cattle, for a few miles out anyway.

The man, at this stage, reached for a rifle hanging from a nail in a post at the end of the table, and shot a wedge-tailed eagle that had come to rest on the shade house containing the bullock's leg.

A further diversion started as the younger girl decided playfully to flick a spoonful of water across the table at her sister, who retaliated with a cupful. Quickly hanging up his rifle, the man joined in by tipping a jugful over them both; the woman, by this time, had brought a dish of water which she proceeded to empty over him. The originator now filled

a bucket and, struggling over with it, poured the water on
her mother. In no time water was cascading from the table,
converting the floor into a lake, and everyone was rapidly
being soaked.

I sat in my Rover watching this amazing family through
the windscreen while they filled anything capable of holding

water and saturated each other. It would evidently save washing up after dinner, which I assumed to be over. Then, as suddenly as it had started, the fight was finished, most of the things having been washed off the table. I thought that here was one of the few households where you could get bogged driving from the lounge to the kitchen by way of the dining-room.

Throughout all this Grandma was clapping and barracking, and now she called me over to ask if I could post a letter for her in the next month or so. I said I'd be glad to, and gave her an envelope she'd asked for. She then wondered if I had a piece of paper that she could write the letter on, so I gave her a pad. I heard her muttering, loud enough for me to hear, that if she had a pencil she could get started, so I handed her one from my bag. After a while she held the letter up proudly and remarked that it would be finished if only she had one of "them stamps" to put on it. Having already anticipated her, and determined to be helpful to the bitter end, I said she would make me very pleased if she would take off my hands this one I happened to have. Before putting the finished product safely away, I was inquisitive enough to notice the real bush classic she had written as an address:

"Master Tommy,
  Care of his father,
    Northern Territory."

As long as they knew his father, I'm sure Master Tommy would receive his letter, through the efficient P.M.G. Department. And, knowing the outback and its people I'm sure that this was very likely the only information required for its safe delivery.

The family were now ready for more talk of this latest excitement coming their way. My camp consisted of a small group I'd named, originally as a joke, "The Gunbarrel Road Construction Party," because whenever possible we liked to make our roads straight. It didn't matter that when we got into the sandhills a more suitable name might have been "The Corkscrew Road Construction Party."

I mentioned we'd be skirting the little-known Gibson's Desert west of the range system six hundred miles from

Alice Springs, and our supplies would have to be brought by our own truck from the nearest place — a return trip of well over a thousand miles. My present camp was a hundred miles away, and I usually went on ahead to make a survey of the route. When finished, this road would be the only one linking east to west across that part of Central Australia.

A native came to the homestead at this point, with a badly swollen, obviously poisoned finger, to ask in broken English for help. Before deciding on a method of treatment we inquired if it hurt him very much. His reply was typical of the outlook the Australian aboriginal usually has about such things: "Him all right, but he keeps on faintin' all the time." After a long course of hot water bathing and some blood-poisoning pills from my kit, with advice to return for more pills from time to time, he went back to his camp, only to lance it himself with a sharp mulga stick. The natives, who make ideal patients, seem to be able to do things like this, which might have a much more serious effect on a white man. A little native girl once came to me with a poisoned thumb, and I was forced to relieve it by giving her an injection through the base of her nail. She didn't move a muscle of her face or arm, and even smiled up at me and said, 'Sankyou,'' as I put a lolly in her small hand afterwards.

The rest of the afternoon was taken up in discussing our new work — how we could help them and they could help us. They could let us have water in unlimited quantities from an unusual spring, only a few feet deep, which never dried up. That immediately explained the apparently careless use of water, during the recent water fight, in a country as noticeably dry as this. I intended to establish a large fuel dump at their station for the future use of the diesel plant as well as the trucks, and was assured this would be quite all right. When I asked about their own supply line, they told me they had a mail truck through now and then, and that it was due now. As this was Wednesday I asked if it was their usual mail day. They told me it was, and they would be expecting it at ten minutes past three. Just as I was thinking how fortunate they were to have such a reliable mail driver, to be able to quote to the minute when he would arrive, they added casually that if he didn't get here then, 'Well, he may not come till Saturday.''

As the evening drew near, with everyone brimming with expectations as to the future, out came the guitar again, accompanied this time by a large banjo, and this happiest of families made the desert come alive to the sound of cowboy songs and very professional yodelling. I was made to join in, although I tried to escape, having more knowledge of my own limitations than they.

That night black clouds gathered and it looked as if we were in for the father of all storms, but this only made them more pleased than ever. I thought their joy was due to the good cattle feed that would result from rain, but in this case it wasn't. It was because it would keep me with them longer. The bottom falls out of that country after a downpour, and a motor vehicle is useless. Grandma went off to bed in high spirits, chuckling and rattling her tin of stones.

Then someone noticed the absence of Miss Guitar. Her mother knew why she had slipped away, for she had admonished her just beforehand for an incorrect note she had played on the instrument, and had forced her to play it several times properly. The storm rumbled ominously, and there was still no reappearance of the girl, so they began to think better of letting her camp out in the sandhills, which had been their first intention.

Taking a kerosene lantern we trooped off into the night in the direction of the aborigines' camp. They had not seen her, but immediately assumed control of the tracking operations. Cutting her tracks by lamplight, and sorting them out from all of ours, they followed them in a twisting pattern for a mile through the sandhills. It was there they found her, asleep under a mulga tree, her tear-stained face buried in her arms.

Being the newcomer in the group, it happened that I was the only one to whom she would listen, so the others retraced their steps to the house with the aid of the natives, leaving the lamp for me. I spoke of what wonderful people

The author, cleaner than usual.

they were, and of how fortunate she was to be a member of such a pleasant family, who took such an interest in her. I told how I'd been camping in the bush for a long time and what a happy surprise it had been for me to have met them that morning. She had been living among native children and in cattle camps all her life and had grown to be one of the truly genuine outdoor girls, found only in the Australian back country. It might have looked a little unusual anywhere else, people creeping about at dead of night rounding up their family, but when we arrived back at the homestead, no one referred to the incident again. A lesson had been learnt, and now all was well.

Relatively early, by city standards, everyone settled down at last. The few drops of rain had not increased as is so often the case with these desert storms, and I lay quietly thinking about the events of half a day in the lives of these newly discovered friends.

Suddenly, as if in answer to my feeling that there could never be a dull moment here, there came a loud explosion from the kitchen. The family were all up in a flash. I groped for my torch before the lamp could be lit, and we went looking for this latest disturbance — the cattleman armed with his rifle, grandma with her tin of stones. On a tea chest we found a newly made cake, lying among some shattered plastic that had been its container. The cake had warmed the plastic, and the few drops of cold rain that followed had placed such undue stress on it that it blew to pieces. We still refer to that as their "Atomic Sponge."

We went back to our well-earned attempts at sleep, and amazingly enough the remainder of the night passed without further entertainment. The morning brought clear, hot skies once more — the "storm" had not even laid the dust.

It was time for me to be on my way back to camp. Assuring them I would soon return with the best turkey's nest dam-making equipment in the north-west, I asked which was the best way out. With the most solemn expression I'd seen since arriving, the man informed me: "Just go straight

Top: Trouble before we even begin. *Bottom:* When the equipment breaks down, the bulldozer has to tow the lot.

on past the chest of drawers, turn left at the wardrobe, and leave the sink on your right. Don't make a sharp turn at the head of the bed and you can't miss it.'' The tracks from the rocking-chair past the dressing table apparently led out only to a windmill.

The hundred miles to my camp were gone before I realized it, although the journey was all across country. I had so much to think about.

The Happy Family's station was on the line from my present starting point, a hundred miles distant, but could be reached at this time only by a very round-about system of existing station tracks. I therefore planned to make a direct link across, thus saving eighty miles return for each supply trip and all subsequent trips necessary for the following weather station construction team. Incidentally, it would open up a new and shorter way for the station people, something that is always welcome. The country in between is nearly all solid mulga scrub, as I found from my reconnaissance; this explained to me why a direct road had never been made before. It is so thick that, in a number of cases, the flat tyres I collected on the way could not be changed where they happened as, owing to the heavy scrub, it was impossible to open the Land-Rover doors. Even to get out of the vehicle, I had to drive on a way.

I never dreamt, at the time, that this particular section of the road would be used for the constant coming and going of tourist coaches on their way to Ayers Rock in the cooler season. Being close to the Northern Territory-South Australian border, it proved a considerably shorter cut to our ''Rock,'' and tourist agencies were quick to realize it. Much later, when I was returning from farther afield, I came on one such bus that had been brought to a sudden stop when the wheel had fallen off. Tourists of all ages were camping everywhere in little tents, waiting for the repairs to be carried out, and they didn't seem over happy at the delay. One woman had a broken denture, which I offered to mend. But after that I hurried away while I was still in their good books and before they found out I had anything to do with making the road.

When I returned to my camp, I found the party had the

machinery serviced and were all ready to go. They asked me how the trip had gone. "Well," I began "there was this Happy Family . . ." Then I shrugged helplessly, giving it up almost before starting. "You'd never believe me anyway."

2

The Formation of the Gunbarrel Road Construction Party

Meeting near the Coober Pedy opal fields, we made the journey to our starting point together. Half the party had come from Adelaide, with the bulldozer on a huge loader, accompanied by the operator and cook; the rest of us arrived on a road we had recently made from Maralinga, near the Nullarbor Plain. This group was made up of our grader driver and his machine, a heavy equipment fitter, a handyman, and myself. We had all been preparing the bomb-testing site before this new work became necessary.

Both sections of our party had received their share of excitement before reaching our meeting place. I had put some trucks and equipment on a goods train at Woomera, and our group, as they often did, had travelled with them. On a trip such as this, meals are cooked alonside the railway line on grilling wire, which is left hanging on a mulga tree for each subsequent trip. The train's endless shunting, backing up, and banging at the sidings leave ample time to make a fire and cook a meal before reboarding. It's not unusual to be awakened at these stops by a goat noisily eating your shirt too close to your ear. And at one of these sidings I woke up just in time to see a shirt sleeve disappearing into a goat's mouth. It was here we had our unrehearsed diversion.

After we had boiled a billy and cooked some chops, a small boy of about eight wanted to sit in one of our big lorries and look at the things we had tied down to several flat-top railway carriages. Only too pleased at his interest, I took him along the train to where our equipment was supposed to be. But I couldn't even find the carriages. We ran to the other side of the train, which was now ready to go, and I couldn't believe my eyes at the scene that greeted me. All our trucks had been shunted off the main line on to the siding, and unhooked. A whistle blew as I raced along to the driver and begged him not to drive the train away until I'd seen the station master. I was told that the train, having taken on a number of water tanks, had become too heavy by law for the track. The tanks were for the people on the waterless Nullarbor Plain, so they'd decided to leave our cars behind.

I said the old hackneyed, "But you can't do that," to which he replied by pointing out the obvious, "I already have," as he waved again to the engine driver. I must have sounded convincingly urgent, however, for the station master agreed to get in touch with the train controller at Port Augusta by phone. I tried to explain the situation to the controller, but I'm sure he didn't believe me when I told him I had to make a road across Australia with this equipment. I went on to say I had arrangements made half-way to Alice Springs and these would be thrown out it they didn't hook our trucks back on the train. Before recovering from his doubt at my story, he at last arranged with the station master and engine driver, who by this time were fuming, to have the trucks recoupled.

The small boy was delighted at the havoc he'd caused as the two-hour delay gave him a longer look at our gear. We let him sit at the wheel of the largest truck as it was shunted about, and he couldn't quite understand why I was so pleased with him.

At the next siding I climbed into my Rover, on its carriage, where I had a radio transmitter installed to check on how the others were getting on with the bulldozer. No sooner had I made contact than the astounding news came over the speaker that they would be delayed a long time before reaching the meeting place. Trying to avoid a cyclist, they had crashed the whole thirty tons of the low loader and tractor into a hotel near Adelaide. They couldn't attempt to remove the prime mover, as it was the only thing now holding up the building. Meanwhile, a second loader was on its way for the transfer of the tractor, leaving the first to prop up the hotel. The driver told the manager that he wasn't really supposed to drop into hotels while on duty — it seemed that this "drive-in" was the first in Adelaide.

As I walked back along the train to relate this latest turn of events to the others, I met the handyman, who said he wanted a few words with me. He had slowly realized just where we were going, and wanted to know if it would put our arrangements out very much if he stayed behind. He explained that he felt he was far too young to die. Although this would leave me short of a driver, I was really very pleased he had told me of his feelings at this stage instead of waiting until we reached a point of no return, so I relieved him of his job there and then and told him we would manage.

At last we reached the Nullarbor Plain, so we again unhooked the carriages, and proceeded to unload our equipment. Travelling with us were a number of men bound for the Maralinga construction camps, and as they disembarked from the train they looked around mournfully. All they saw was a flat, bare, simmering horizon which so depressed them that, mumbling something about how you could see a bull ant for ten miles, they tried to get straight back on the the train. I overheard one say, "Well, at least you can see when the boss is coming."

To the clicking of every official camera in the area, we at last moved away from Maralinga on our way to meet the others. One vehicle, for want of a driver, was bolted, with its front wheels removed, to a fitting we had just welded to the rear of the grader.

The first night out it rained so heavy and unexpectedly that one member estimated he wrung thirty gallons of water out of his pillow and blankets next morning. Whenever it rains, or even looks like rain, in Central Australia, the centipedes, accompanied by the scorpions, come out of hiding, and it was a very tired group which got under way that day, through lack of sleep searching for them. I found them in my boots after carrying our a routine check before putting them on.

I was beginning to think that this project could only improve with age. There's always a bright side, however, because if everthing is running well, then the only change that can occur is one for the worse. In this case, all we could look forward to was a rosy future, even though at the time it was difficult to convince everyone of this.

As unbelievable as it at first appeared, we all met at the arranged place near Coober Pedy, and the Gunbarrel Road Construction Party came into being. It eventuated that the grader driver and cook stayed with me for the next eight years: the bulldozer driver's little daughter made up his mind for him after six. We had obtained the services of a new handyman, and he was to provide us with many episodes of unscheduled entertainment in the years to follow.

The one who was to be the long range supply driver had been with me off and on for nine years already in many very remote and difficult situations, so I was sure of his continued faithful services; coming originally from Ireland he had a suitable approach to any problem likely to arise. If he didn't want to go anywhere, he would use such Irishisms as, "You can include me out." The cook had been a former shearer's cook, and had lived in the bush all his life; he had an exceptionally calm and quiet temperament, and a good measure of bush humour in his make-up. Because of the long periods he spent alone on his machine, the grader driver was always called "Grader Garbo." He had been operating a road grader for many years on the country roads of South Australia, and had gained valuable knowledge of the mechanical side of his job. The main heavy equipment fitter was recruited for this job because of his specialized experience in the many technical details surrounding the smooth operating and repairs of earth-moving plant. He came on loan from another department, and got us out of many holdups caused by mechanical trouble.

For those people who have a reason, as we had, for entering or passing through aboriginal reserves, it is necessary by law to have a medical examination first. We only learnt this, however, when we were on our way, so we had to arrange it before going on. A radio call to Woomera set the organization in motion for a doctor to be flown the two hundred and fifty miles out to us. We were at a local station watching the cowboys breaking in some wild horses when the plane appeared and circled over the horse yards, much to the disturbance of the already quivering animals, one of which injured a rider against the rail. I told him how lucky he was that the plane had brought a doctor, but as we pulled him out quickly from under the low bottom rail, he made no effort to conceal the fact that he was entirely unconvinced.

Our dog managed to ferret out a large sand goanna during the ensuing examination, which was conducted at our camp — in a tent open at both ends. Just as the doctor adjusted his stethoscope, dog and goanna headed for the tent, the goanna leading the way at a terrific rate through the awning, between the medical officer and the unfortunate horse-breaker, with the dog a yard behind. The black bag went flying, and it looked for a while as if the trembling doctor was about to direct the receiving end of the stethoscope against himself. After the animals had gone he retrieved his bag and, shutting it with a snap, confirmed shakily that we were all fit to go anywhere, and that he would take care of the paper work on his return to Woomera. He added, as he hustled back to the plane, that he wouldn't pass himself for the job.

Now, at last, it seemed we could travel together as a complete unit to where our unusual project was to start. It was comparative civilization on the Alice Springs road to the border. Some travellers on this road might hesitate at the use of the word civilization, but to us it could just as well have been Broadway.

By the time we had pulled all the plant off the road to camp that night, I had managed to kill two snakes, and had them tied to a rail on the Rover for everyone to see. I noticed that no one slept on the ground after seeing them, but opened their swag rolls along the seats of the bulldozer

and grader as high up as possible.

There were three trucks: one full of bulk rations, one for the transport of fuel and water and all the oils and greases needed for the machinery, and the third was intended for use as a supply line for everything. We then had two Land-Rovers, one fitted out as a mobile workshop carrying oxy-welding equipment, vice, and tools, and the other I'd had especially made up as a survey wagon. To mention a few of the items on it — a theodolite and tripod with stopwatches and calculation books for astronomical fix-ations, a radio transceiver also capable of receiving time signals needed for star observations, axe, shovel, mechan-ical spares and tools, a comprehensive outfit for emergency dental work and first aid, rifle, revolver, and hair clippers. One becomes quite good at packing in the bush, whether loading a vehicle or pack camel. The modifications on this survey wagon were the result of experience gained after many years of what is known as bushbashing, or pushing a vehicle through scrub. As most of the trips lasted for five months twice a year much was learnt of the vehicle's per-formance, and improvements were carried out after each expedition.

I'd had the road grader since it was new, to prepare vari-ous testing sites after a survey nine years before, and it was still in use with the same party. Having graded over four thousand miles of our subsequent new roads, much of this several times during the construction as well as later, it could be estimated conservatively that this machine has graded over thirty thousand miles of road. The tractor, which had bulldozed down the hotel, was one of many hired from another department for our use. This often had to be unloaded in order to pull the rest of the plant through sandy creek beds, and then reloaded on its float. A small refriger-ator trailer and water-tank carrier completed the convoy, which had a thousand-mile trip to do before even starting on the work in hand.

We considered it more of a privilege than a job of work, to have been given the opportunity of doing something which had not as yet been attempted.

As we came to one section of the main road with heavy

scrub on either side, we saw it was becoming boggy. Then around a curve, blocking the way, was one of the largest trucks I'd ever seen stuck down to its bumper bar in the mud. It was at least three feet deep, and so was its trailer with its load of a second lighter lorry. The rain we had encountered at the centipede camp must have been widespread. Where the timber is thickest, there is generally a depression any water will lodge in after rain, and the resulting intensity of growth makes it impossible to by-pass an obstruction such as this. There was not a soul in sight. So, starting the bulldozer and driving it off the float once more, we attached a logging-winch cable to the stranded mountain of a vehicle and pulled it, and its trailer, out bodily. Once we had it moving we towed it well clear of the mud to a rise high and dry off the road, leaving it parked neatly in a stony clearing.

This left a crater in the main road, which we repaired by bulldozing in dry dirt and stones from the rise. After compacting it with the dozer and grading it smooth, this turned out to be one of the best parts of the main road, allowing our own convoy to press on as if nothing had happened. The driver of this outfit, I heard later, had seen at a glance what a hopeless plight he had got himself into, so he walked forty miles to the next homestead, caught their mail truck to the railway a further hundred miles away and went to his boss and resigned. The owner of the transport had been surprised to see his driver arrive in a taxi cab, but he was even more surprised when informed of the whereabouts of the truck. "Eight hundred miles away clean out of sight in a bog." I often wondered just what this owner must have thought when, on going to salvage his property, he found it waiting alongside the road with no sign of a bog in sight.

That night, as we settled down for the evening on an open stony plain, I thought that nothing more could possibly happen to anyone on one trip. How wrong I was! At midnight, with everything quiet and our fire flickering its last, headlights appeared on the starlit skyline, As they neared the camp, a car slowed to a stop. I was fully awake by now, and, as I was nearest the road, a man carrying a torch approached me. He told me they were tourists on their way to the Northern Territory and hadn't seen a stick of wood for miles where they could stop and camp. They wondered if they could boil a billy of water on our fire, which we had made with some sticks we carried with us. Telling him they were very welcome, I asked him to bring his passengers over and make use of the table and lamp. As I stirred up the fire he brought his wife and baby over. I thought as it was late they might like to camp here, so mentioned it as I handed them our tin of tea leaves. They were very pleased with the suggestion, and he set about erecting a small tent while his wife prepared their meal.

Everything went smoothly until the baby stirred, reminding them that it too was hungry. Encouraged by our friendly manner, the woman ventured to ask a question which had probably been in her mind since she first sighted our fire. Could she possibly bath her baby? Assuming they had a tub and the sort of thing necessary for such an operation, I assured her we could supply water, that it wasn't too late, and that it would be a perfect opportunity. I asked if there was anything I could do to help. The baby looked pretty clean to me, but as we weren't very good judges, I just followed instructions while her husband finished preparing the tent for what was left of the night. The washing up over, I put on another billy to supply more hot water.

It seemed she didn't have a tub, as she wanted to know if we had anything that could be used. I offered her a mixing bowl, not wanting to appear at a loss, and realizing it was the most presentable item among our utensils. Out of politeness, I'm sure she would have used the camp oven, but I knew nobody bathed babies in camp ovens. She seemed pleased, but when I brought it out from the ration truck it was smaller than I had imagined. In fact it didn't look quite as large as the baby. Apologizing for our lack of baby-bathing equipment, and explaining that we did not need it very often, I was relieved to hear her say what a lovely dish it was, and just right. Here we were, at past midnight, in the open plains, getting a bath ready for a baby — a bird's eye view of the scene might have appeared just a little odd!

She now declared the water to be ready, after first testing it with her elbow, and asked if I would hold the infant while she prepare the bowl. Up until now I'd been trying my best, but here was something different. I must have been holding the baby like a theodolite, because she assured me it wouldn't break. Then came the actual bathing. As I feared, the baby wouldn't quite fit in the bowl, so I suggested putting one end in at a time. I held the baby while she used the cotton wool and little sticks with knobs on the ends — I was glad she carried *something* with her. We could have had a go at making even those, I supposed, as I watched, fascinated. Then it was time to end-for-end it, but after that it was still dry in the middle, I took the practical approach to this problem by pointing out that it could be overcome if I were to put a bit of a bend in the baby to help it to fit. This worked half its diameter, and outside bend coping with the remainder.

Throughout all this the baby didn't murmur, but as I put it down on a coloured rug it looked up at me with an expression that clearly said, "Thank heaven that's over." The husband came over as his wife dusted and rolled up their child, and announced that all was ready for them to turn in. I felt relief next morning when I saw the baby still breathing and gurgling; it must have been stronger than I'd imagined. The family set off again, after an early breakfast, before everyone had got up. Our handyman, who had slept late, said he dreamt he'd heard a baby crying during the night.

We caused great excitement when at last we rolled into the homestead planned to be our starting point. The children were immediately all over everything, and watched wide-eyed the process of unloading the big bulldozer for the last time. From here it was on its own, and the float received a well-earned servicing for its return to Adelaide free of the weight on its back.

Introductions and explanations were made over afternoon tea. The station people found it hard to believe that the normally quiet atmosphere of their routine was to be changed, but at the same time they were pleased enough. It would be easier for them to reach parts of their own property, now only accessible on horseback.

The next day saw the last of the float, and work was begun on the maintenance of the plant in readiness for our project. It seemed odd that, before starting even, much work of this kind was needed, and I wondered what it would be like at the finish. It was during these operations that I set out on the reconnaissance for the first section, and found the Happy Family.

On my return, and as a goodwill gesture for the help we'd received, we used the bulldozer to make a truck-loading pit, and a small swimming pool in a dry creek-bed for the children. If it ever rained some water might collect in it, and the overflow from a windmill could help. They might get a swim in it one day, but as we were told it had rained an average of only two inches a year for eleven years, we were doubtful.

Our actual work on the project started the next day, bulldozing right outside the homestead, while the station owner's wife photographed the historic event with her small home-movie camera. We were to see the film later, after spending an afternoon helping to mend the projector.

The making of the first road across Central Australia had begun.

3

An Introduction to Central Australia

Until our project, there had never been any road access in the area bounded by the Nullarbor Plain in the south, the latitude of Broome and Halls Creek nine hundred miles north, the road bisecting Australia through Alice Springs, and the longitude of 122 degrees in the vicinity of Broome, southerly to Carnegie cattle station, the most eastern and remote homestead in central Western Australia.

Due to this complete absence of roads, and of surface water, this area of more than six hundred and thirty thousand square miles had only been entered by a handful of hardy explorers. In the early part of this century surveyor Canning and his party located his remarkable stock route, and later a few venturesome missionaries and stockmen settled around the fringes.

Just how iron-willed these men must have been can be realized only by someone who has had to battle with this country over a long period of time. A short trip cannot give very much indication of the underlying thoughts and feelings that surround camps and expeditions, for these don't develop until prolonged hardship has been endured. Such things as the memory of one vivid sunset, seen from a place where no white man has ever been, is enough to keep an explorer going long after all regard for personal comfort has been abandoned. It is the anticipation of discovery, possibly more that the discovery itself, that is the strong factor governing these men, and encouraging them to continue despite inhospitable surroundings.

Much has been written about the fight for survival of the aboriginal tribes of Central Australia, but here again without personal contact with the problems involved the magnitude of their fight cannot be fully appreciated. To read of heat, hunger, and thirst while sitting in a cool house, alongside a well-stocked pantry, and within reach of a water tap that never runs dry, cannot possibly bring more than a sympathetic comment. But if the reader has experienced such things himself, he can understand how value out of all proportion can be placed on the seemingly worthless. For example, to the white man, a three-foot length of fencing wire, to hand at the right time and place, can assume importance in the extreme; a rusty axe head is a treasure to the native. This general approach to everything comes to bushmen both black and white, and is in the basic characteristics of the explorer.

The country of Central Australia can be divided up into four types; sand ridges covered with thick mulga scrub, sand ridges among mountain ranges, sand ridges covered with spinifex, and bare sand ridges.

Bordering the northern edge of the Nullarbor Plain are the sand ridges covered with mulga. These extend for five hundred miles east to west without a break, and the belt is two hundred miles wide. The ridges are parallel, often only fifty yards apart, and a single ridge can be a hundred miles long. They average forty feet in height, and their southern face is the steeper. Travelling from north to south is almost feasible, therefore, whereas in most instances the reverse is impossible except on foot. The mulga trees are up to twelve feet high, casting about twenty per cent shade, and are extremely old for their size, being hardy enough to survive each five-month-long scorching summer.

During a drought in the cattle country, where mulga is

Top: To make an airfield we needed a more permanent camp than usual. *Bottom:* Our bush dentistry even included anaesthetic.

often found, stock can live on the herbage. Here and there are small patches, not more that a mile across, of she-oak, indicating the sure presence of a limestone ground surface in that area, which in turn means higher country. This region is also relieved by occasional salt lakes, varying in size from very small to many miles in diameter. Very close to these, the regular pattern of the sand ridges is disturbed; they are converted into confused mountains of sand which are very often quite bare and move about with the wind. The lakes are mostly bottomless blue mud with a thin coating of white salt, and must be avoided at all costs. I was hopelessly bogged for a week at a time during my early contacts with them, as they look so invitingly smooth after months of pushing over sandhills and through dense mulga.

Claypans on which heavy aircraft can land without previous preparation of any kind are also to be found, and can be driven over without danger, Although they can be distinguished by their red colour, in some cases it pays to check before venturing on to them. When water is found by drilling near these claypans and salt lakes, it is invariably undrinkable and often as briny as sea water, even when struck at a depth of fifty feet. There is a perfect example of colloidal suspension of clay in any rain water which collects on their surface, and which adds another wafer-thin floor when it has evaporated, explaining the way in which these pans are originally formed. It will not clear or settle when the water is left in a container for weeks, but in an emergency a sprinkling of white ashes from a fire will make it usable. A collecting hole must be dug under the water, as it is rarely more than an inch deep, and this will fill by draining a large area. I once came upon a dry claypan after dark, and camped on it at one end. It was a clear starry night, but next morning I woke to find myself surrounded by water. I was amazed until it occurred to me that a slight breeze must have come up in the night and eased the remaining water, which was apparently still on the far end of the claypan, along to my end, which shows how exactly

Top: The cook at work in an overnight camp.
Bottom: Camped on the edge of the Gibson Desert.

level these claypans are. On a salt lake, however, rain will seep in, rendering the surface more treacherous than ever. I have heard that farther east a complete camel wagon slowly went out of sight in one.

Saltbush and bluebush seem to accompany mulga as a ground herbage, while spinifex keeps nearer mallee.

This country gave me the most valuable experience for vehicle modification. It was here that, during more than five years, research for a suitable vehicle was automatically carried out in conjuction with my work. Each year new weaknesses became evident, and our ever helpful but harassed workshops at headquarters managed to cope with my latest discoveries and suggestions.

The northern edge of this most heart-breaking section of Australia is reasonably well defined. The "sand ridge among mountain range" type takes over and the mulga gives way to a greater variety of plants. Also the intensity of both sand ridges and general foliage eases, and spinifex predominates.

Spinifex is a vegetation closely resembling darning needles, growing in spherical clumps from several inches to six feet in diameter. These spheres are separate from each other, leaving quite bare, clean, sandy patches in between. The distance between each plant varies with different types of spinifex — of which many are found — there being ample walking space between the largest clusters, whereas the smaller they are the closer they are together. It was often referred to by the early explorers as the "Deadly trioda," using a portion of its botanical name, as the fetlocks of horses and camels became raw and bleeding as they brushed through it. In the mid-year season long, straw-like shoots with ears of grain, like a prairie of cultivated wheat, emerge from the clusters. Stock thrives on this and horses take on a healthy glister after feeding on it for a period. These heads don't last long, but in a good year the growth is above eye level; nothing can be seen beyond the bonnet of a vehicle when driving through it, and for direction total reliance must be placed on a compass. Within minutes, the husks clog radiator cores, even though a fine screen is used, and make it necessary to clean them out many times an hour.

I thought I had a wonderful idea, after a particularly inconvenient day of this, but my hopes were dulled by the fitter next day when he informed me that "blow back" fans had already been invented.

Spinifex, however green it looks, will ignite in seconds, owing to the presence in it of resinous gum, quickly becoming a raging inferno giving off dense clouds of black smoke and intense heat. The fury in each cluster is shortlived, but it is enough to light the next one, and so on; with a wind behind it, the fire can continue on out of sight. Small lizards are always to be seen darting from clump to clump, and natives secure them for food by burning off great areas to drive them out. The presence and location of a tribe are often indicated by volumes of black smoke wafting skyward, visible for many miles. The gum is separated from the spinifex by a method developed by the natives, and used for moulding their spear throwers or woomera handles, or patching holes in wooden dishes. While the gum is still pliable as a knob on the woomera handles, they can insert it in a sharp chip of stone which is used as a chisel after the whole thing has hardened. Spinifex is really a blessing in disguise. It breaks springs in winter, boils radiators in summer, reduces you to one big ache at the end of a day's drive over it, and pierces your ankles as you walk through it. But without the deadly trioda, which covers all of Central Australia, we would quickly have the infinitely worse condition of a bare and desolate sandy desert, blown about at will by the equinoctial gales.

In place of the reduced quantity of mulgas, this section of country has park-like regions of straight-trunked desert oaks which have their only foliage at the top, about twenty feet up, and provide full shade, The trunks, averaging a foot in diameter, have rough black bark and are, as everything has to be in this country, tough. Resembling cork, and easily cut with a pocket knife, the bark of the corkwood trees that grow in the desert oak areas burns to a clean, fine white ash. The presence of a sugary substance among the foliage is indicated to the native children by small ants, and they chew it as a sweet. Bloodwoods add to the variety, and these heal quickly when chopped, with the bleeding and hardening of the red gum that oozes out. Then come what are possibly the most beautiful of all the gums, the well-known ghost gums — a dream come true for the artist or the colour photographer. In some seasons of the year they produce a snow-white, chalk-like powder, which leaves on the smooth bark a thin film covering even the smallest branch. This will come off to the touch, and the contrast with the healthy bright green of the leaves is then shown at its striking best. As well as in creek beds, they flourish in the most unlikely places, such as high on a steep, rocky slope of a mountain.

This country sounds like a paradise when the wild peach trees are then described with their fruit, which can be made into a pie or eaten as it is. But don't be misled. The fruit of the quandong trees, as they are called, is the size of a large marble with a seed, which is used in the game of checkers, almost as big. It ripens to a bright red in the late spring, and a grove of such trees looks like a cultivated orchard.

The mountain range system occupies the eastern half of this two hundred-mile-wide region, and terminates abruptly with the western end of the Rawlinson Range, where the Gibson Desert takes over. Giles, who in 1874 was the first to explore the area, named the Gibson Desert after the first white man to lose his life there, and it is probably some of the most inhospitable country of the outback.

Gibson was a member of Giles's party of four, the others being Tietkens and Andrews. They were all camped at a base near a water rock hole at the newly named Rawlinson Range, and were waiting for rain before attempting a trip farther to the west. When no change in the weather came for a long time, Giles thought he would try anyway. Against his better judgment, he left his usual mainstay of the party, Tietkens, in the camp when Gibson persuaded Giles to allow him to go instead. They got about sixty miles, left a small supply of water and dried horse meat in a mulga tree, and sent loose two pack horses to find their own way back to base along the tracks. After struggling on another sixty miles westerly, in intense heat, it became obvious, after the horse Gibson was riding collapsed from thirst, that to continue was out of the question. So they turned back, and the two desperate men spelled each other by alternately riding and walking. In a bid to speed up the return, and considering himself to be possessed of the greater endurance of the two, Giles sent Gibson riding on ahead to base, to get Tietkens to return for him. Meanwhile he endeavoured to shorten the distance on foot. Gibson was to use part of the horse meat and water left in the tree, leaving the remainder for Giles if he could reach it before help came.

My impression of this arrangement is that it was a misguided self-sacrifice on the part of Giles. He often mentions in his diary that Gibson was unreliable because of his inexperience, and in such a situation, it might be thought he would have kept this in mind and made a rescue surer for both by going himself. The task of following tracks freshly made, without becoming lost, seemed easy enough but that was the last anyone saw of Gibson. The first two horses sent back to base had wandered away from their own tracks, which is unusual for horses, but they were probably crazed with thirst. These second tracks were the ones Gibson followed, in error. Giles realized this after finally struggling to the junction of the two, on an examination of the tracks, and he knew then that help would not be coming. With the water container on his back, holding the meagre supply left after Gibson had used it, Giles now had to almost crawl the rest of the way to base if he were to survive and begin looking for Gibson. He was to do it by drawing to the utmost on his nearly spent reserves.

After the day it took for him to be able to move again, he and Tietkens went in search of Gibson. Reaching the wrong set of tracks and pursuing them, they found that he must have caught sight of a range of hills, and branched off once again towards them, thinking them to be the Rawlinsons, but in effect he would have been travelling in almost the opposite direction away from the base. Gibson, although he had the only compass left, could not have checked with it first, and, being now in the grip of panic, terror, and thirst for a certainty, had wandered to a horrible death in the sandhills. His would-be rescuers followed him to a point beyond which there would surely be no returning, and were forced back to base once more, hoping that a merciful death would quickly claim him, and so put him out of the agony they were themselves experiencing. It must have been with a heavy heart that Giles made the note in his diary that this desolate region west of the Rawlinsons was now to be known as the Gibson Desert.

As near as I can ascertain, my final location for the road we were about to make, and which now exists, passes the spot where the search for Gibson was ultimately abandoned. I had reason later to know exactly how he must have felt in his last hours of consciousness.

For want of a better name, somebody called the remainder of our area to the north "The Great Sandy Desert," as it is composed in the main of the "sand ridges covered with spinifex" type of country. This region is almost completely devoid of trees, leaving the wider valleys between the ridges quite open and making a route parallel to them comparativly easy to negotiate. But a course set across them, say to the north-north-east, would be virtually impossible with anything short of a camel or an aeroplane, as it would be fraught with thousands of sand-ridge crossings.

The climatic conditions in this country can easily be classified. From November to March it is searingly hot and dry; April, June, and July have ideal temperatures but it is dry; August and September are dry with seemingly never-ending winds, and it appears to be fairly dry in October. It might be a little unjust to say it is all that dry, because for some years we have had up to two inches of rain. After a cycle of about twelve years, six inches can be expected. But clear skies will be seen for most of the year. To quote one small boy's answer to an examination question, "The climate of Central Australia in summer is such that its inhabitants have to live elsewhere."

The unpleasantness of even a slight contact with a blanket has forced me to get up around midnight and try to cool down with a wet cloth, and even then the temperature has been over the century. I know I wished I were elsewhere.

In the winter month of July, on the other hand, the water in the tank taps freezes solid, and where it lies protected from the sun in deep boot tracks, white frost can be seen until mid morning. The days, however, probably could not be improved on anywhere.

By far the most disturbing period of the whole year fol-

lows the winter, with a succession of gales, making camping out in the open most disconcerting. Our cook is obliged to hold down the billy lids and pots with rocks of varying sizes, and in some areas he carries a collection of them. Some days he only needs to use his twenty-knot model, while on others he has to struggle over to the small stove with his fifty-knot pot-lid rocks. The winds come laden with sand or fine dust, and often our canvas awning is torn and then ripped to shreds with us perhaps still inside, holding one hand over our eyes, the other covering a mug of tea. The winds can take one completely unawares and once, while making some survey cakes, a particularly unpleasant gale hit us. Afterwards it seemed we had discovered a novel way of making double-sided sandpaper. When the gales hit during the night, we almost have to dig ourselves out next morning from the sand and dirt heaped on our beds, only to find the awning flattened with everthing swept from the table and broken. We find the bread-tin lids and frying-pans by determining the direction of the wind and driving on a reverse compass bearing through the bush for anything up to half a mile.

I once saw a duststorm coming while alone on a reconnaissance survey in an open vehicle. Whereas a piece of paper would have fallen vertically if dropped just before the storm struck, I don't think an anvil would have touched ground a moment later. I was suddenly in the midst of the most violent outback storm I had ever encountered. The sun was obliterated by a dense fog of red dirt and, as midday turned to night in the space of a minute, I pressed a towel over my face in order to breathe, After four hours I began to wonder when it was going to ease as I huddled down under the windscreen. I was still wondering the same thing two days later. Hungry and grimy, I decided that there must be easier ways of earning a living. I shall never forget the relief I experienced when the storm eventually stopped. At last I could eat something, and have a drink of water.

These experiences have all happened at around the same time of year, so we look forward to having September behind us, even though temperatures in the hundred and twenties are on the way. We then wish it were cold again, as do all humans, who are difficult to keep satisfied.

As a rule, rabbits are few and far between and sometimes we don't see even one for years. During very severe droughts near areas where they are more common, however, I have seen them climb to the topmost branches of a mulga tree to eat the herbage there. At first glance, we thought we'd found a koala farm.

Although there are a few kangaroos in this country, they are not often found, and a year's work can be done without more than half a dozen being seen.

Dingo tracks cover our freshly made road each morning in most areas, but we rarely see the animal. And, although we have often noticed wild camel tracks superimposed upon tracks made by us the previous evening, we have only seen one camel in this part of the country. I had been flashing a mirror to the bulldozer driver two miles away to give him his next direction, when I casually looked behind me. A long neck protruded from a small bush, and a pair of eyes with a supercilious expression in them peered down over a long nose at me. The start I received must have shortened my life by six months. No visible body or legs; just a bush with a neck.

Before this we were not very sure of the exact construction of a camel's foot, and once, after finding fresh pad marks the size of a dinner plate over our new road made only an hour before, we decided to track down and photograph their maker. In half an hour's time the tracks seemed to be getting fainter and then they disappeared altogether, so we just had to walk back, unsuccessful. When later I studied the tracks of "the neck," I discovered that we'd been tracking our previous one the wrong way, and so the quarry and its pursuers had drawn farther apart every minute.

With the training they get in this country, these animals seem to be able to exist without water for considerable periods — some even indefinitely. We've found the odd kangaroo in places it has taken us weeks to reach in vehicles, and where there has only been a horizon of dry sandhills. Even knowing how kangaroos can travel great distances, we never fail to marvel that they survive.

Wedge-tailed eagles, with wingspans of six feet, which occasionally hover over us hoping one of us might drop, have an advantage over the earthbound, and don't draw undue comment. But the small finches have more of a task to cover the great distances to water, and the frail grey birds, one and a half inches long, are present in their thousands at any unusual seepage. There is one bird-call very familiar throughout Central Australia, sending out the word "is" in morse code continually. A visiting scientist from England asked me what the bird was called. Not really knowing, I told him "the *is* bird." I forgot the incident, but he must have been thinking about if for days because he asked me later what was the reason for its odd name. Another bird practises the Tonic Sol-fa for hours beginning with the high note, continuing for the next two, and finishing with the fifth. It would drive a musically minded listener to an early grave, waiting in vain to hear that fourth note.

Emu tracks are also around but, as is the case with many birds, we rarely see the emu itself. I did see one once, however, in thick scrub, after firing a flare pistol in lieu of the mirror flash on the bulldozer. It suddenly sprang up in a flurry of feathers and raced off into the bush as if pursued by demons. I went to where it had been sitting and found seven still warm eggs. Not having the heart to disturb them, I put a bend in the road especially to by-pass the nest. This is known as Emu Egg Bend, but from an inspection of the eggs next morning I could have saved myself the trouble. They were still there, but had not been revisited by the mother and were white with frost and just as cold. Another time when an emu track was clearly visible in the dried mud of a claypan, I was asked by a team from England what had made it; after telling them, the site for the first atomic tests in Australia was given the name of Emu Field.

We had better luck with another mother bird and her nest of eggs. They had been in a small bush complete with the little bird still sitting, but when the noise of the bulldozer grew louder she became frightened and flew away. Her particular selection for a home was in a sand saddle narrow enough for only the road, so we carefully dug up the whole bush, nest and all, and replanted it half-way up the sandhill. As we passed along the road next day, we noticed, to our delight and satisfaction at our house removal system, that the mother was chirping from her nest as if nothing had happened.

At different times varieties of plagues arrive and flourish in the most desolate places. A loop worm plague was one of these, the worms coming in tens of millions and covering everything. When walking, or whatever name could be given to their progress, they resembled the Greek capital Omega, and showed how they received their name. They appeared in shovelfuls on the windscreen of the Rover, even after a relatively short journey of "bush bashing," giving me an ideal arena on which to study their characteristics. From a quarter of an inch long and as thin as a pin, they increase in size to the thickness of an inch long nail. A cluster of four little pads at each end forms what legs they have, and while one cluster holds on to any surface, the other waves about in search of a landing ground the length of the worm distant. Then the following end attaches itself against and behind the front one, thus forcing the middle into a loop, before the first part sets out once again. They must be unable to see because they are unafraid of any obstacle placed in their path, and merely use it for their next landing ground. With one end anchored, and searching with the other, they fight each other violently if contact is made with a neighbour in a similar stance, which is frequent in their numbers, and wave about in fury striking their opponent with all the force at their command. I watched for hours in the hope of seeing two join up in a reef knot.

Another type of invasion comes in the form of hairy caterpillars, all a little over an inch long. They crawl along, head touching tail, in winding lines up to ten yards long, and it becomes obvious that only their leader has the compass. When we have taken one out of the middle and replaced it quickly with the leader as it diverges from the rest on a course of its own, refusing to have another in front of it. The front of the original line is left to mill around in confusion not knowing where to go. Again, if one is rudely removed from the middle of the column and not replaced at all, the rear portion will stop as if someone had pulled the communication cord, which is in fact the case. They leave behind them, as they march along the sand, a silken-like thread of the same material with which they ultimately build their home. This is built in the form of a pear-shaped, silver-webbed bag, hanging from a tree branch, and in it they will hibernate, all huddled up together. The bag is only four inches long by about two inches in diameter, and the whole line enters it. We used to wonder what would happen if the one in the centre sneezed. Another experiment we tried was to guide the leader around to the tail of the line to form a circle. They did not, however, go around for ever in the same spot as we thought they would, because, as we discovered, the caterpillar leader has a mind of its own.

No description of the back country of Australia could ever be complete without reference to the flies. They cannot be called a plague, because plagues go away, but when millions of things come and stay, then life just gets lonely without them. Sitting in my Rover one day, plotting on a map where our latest length of road came while awaiting the arrival of the bulldozer, I suddenly realized that my personal cloud of flies, which had been with me all along, was slowly growing in intensity. As I was vaguely wondering why, a cough caused me to jump a foot and drop the protractor. A native had crept silently up to my window, bringing his own cloud along, and this had joined mine. It was rather hot that day so I got out of the vehicle to talk with him and also to give our flies more room. I forgot to put on my hat, but I didn't miss it as I stood in the shade thrown by the double cloud of flies. I still wonder if the aboriginal retained his original lot or departed with a mixture.

Termites, or white ants, make their presence known in a very big way for such small creatures. Wood is their favourite main course, but the great variety of their diet shows them to be the least particular of all the inhabitants of our bush. They settle down to an entrée of leather, followed by masonite and lead with canvas on the side, and as if that didn't mildly surprise their waiter, they finish up by devouring a generous helping of concrete. It appears to the layman observer that they have an extremely potent fluid which they use for systematically demolishing man-made structures, and as mortar for carrying out huge construction projects of their own. Their better-known achievements are the blocks of flats rising out of the dry ground to well over skyscraper proportions in comparison to the size of their engineers — anything up to fifteen feet high and ten feet through. The larger of these are solid enough to stop a bulldozer in its tracks, and the smaller ones will resist the attack of a heavy truck.

Another colony prefers to live in a built-up area closely resembling a collection of playing cards stuck on their ends in the sand; the "cards" are three to four feet high, three feet wide, and only a few inches thick. The most wonderful feature of these is the direction of the centre line passing through each one, not only all exactly parallel but placed precisely along their respective local meridians.

When seen from the east or west the settlement takes on the appearance of a continuous wall of hard clay, but the whole structure seems to vanish when viewed end on. Just how they accurately determine their meridian in the first place remains one of our unsolved mysteries. My own theory is that because the hottest period of the day is noon when the sun is north, in order to be least exposed to the sun's rays at the time the thinnest edges point that way. Had they put them at right angles the maximum blast of the sun's heat would be absorbed all day long. I wondered if only one surveyor was commissioned for the entire project, or if each magnetic ant-hill, as they are called, had one of its own, but this point may have been cleared up by the human experts who study them. As the hills are yards apart, the separate surveys certainly checked if the latter was the case, which is probably more likely.

Another type of dwelling evolved by these termites is in beds under the ground. To make these they start at the surface and work down, gradually solidifying the sand to an extremely compact mass the consistency of iron, and of spherical proportions a yard in diameter. These are by far our greatest worry in making a road surface in this country, as a bulldozer blade can only lift them out intact, leaving a large crater that has to be filled in with softer material. Trucks sink deeper in these spots, and make a permanent depression unless worked on again later; if, however, the ant-bed is left in, it withstands traffic wear for ever, and the immediate surroundings become softer and sink down instead. Along some stretches of our roads there may be great distances where the beds are only a matter of feet apart, and the ones we have been able to smooth out have taken an enormous amount of work with a ripper. We were obliged to do the work, in these instances, for the good of the truck travelling back and forth with our supplies on a future project farther out.

A piece of three-ply wood I once left for a few days was converted into a piece of two-ply, the middle ply being completely replaced by termites, I saw another example of their work in an outback bush residence I visited. The roof seemed rather low — you had to bend over almost double in one place to move about — and I remarked to the old bushman owner how inconvenient it must be for him. He explained his serious problem to me as he sat on a box covered with a chaff bag. "It's them white ants," he said slowly, studying the dirt floor. "As they chew the bottom orf me posts, me roof gets lower and lower."

This, then, is the country over which our little party of half a dozen has laid a network of more than four thousand miles of road.

4

It Never Rains But It Pours

Before I start the actual story of our project, let me tell of one occasion, much earlier, which shows the way troubles in every shape or form never seem to come to us singly, but often build up over a free period and descend on us all at once. We often thought this must be more than just coincidence.

On this occasion, Bill, our fuel and supplies driver, and I went off on our own into the desert to prepare for another job which was later to develop into headline news throughout the world. One completely dissociated and almost disastrous event followed another so frequently that our ultimate end on this planet seemed inevitable, or so we thought at the time.

We were about to leave our headquarters in Adelaide for the desert site I had chosen for the project in hand during a recent expedition that had involved several months of lone bush bashing and exploration. The first thing, as always, was to try to find water there, and with this in view we had negotiated with the Department of Mines for a small boring plant, and had selected a heavy truck from our own transport section to carry it. We could have chosen any truck from several dozen available, and we took one which appeared to suit. From that moment our troubles began.

It was a Friday afternoon, and I drove off to the Adelaide depot, only fourteen miles away, to fetch the drilling rig waiting to be loaded with a crane. As we planned to be on our way over the week-end, Bill Lloyd, the driver, had taken my Rover to finalize his affairs and left me his truck, which had two petrol tanks, so in the hurry before knock-off time he did not bother to top them up. After all, it was only fourteen miles.

Six miles along the way the engine started to falter from lack of fuel, so I gratefully switched the tap to the other tank. It soon proved to be bone dry. After coasting to the side of the highway out of the stream of traffic, I managed to hitch-hike to a phone box several miles away and summoned headquarters to come to my aid with a couple of tins of petrol. By the time I reached the depot everyone was about to leave for the week-end, but first they lifted the boring plant on to the truck.

The plant was supposed to be a mobile piece of equipment in the bush, but here in the city, up on a truck, it looked most cumbersome. During the slow crawl through the peak-hour traffic, with many stops to check for clearance of doubtful electric wires, there were many impatient honks of car horns and caustic remarks from irate drivers bent on getting home.

Next morning Bill and I exchanged vehicles, filled up with petrol, and started out for our first goal — Woomera. This is normally a day's trip, but we didn't arrive there for more than a week. It soon started to rain and after only a hundred and forty miles, when we drew off the road to change a flat tyre, our heavy truck with its huge load bogged down two yards away from the bitumen highway. We had to camp there overnight, and only got under way again with the help of another large road transport which towed us out; we continued on with the large vehicle in the lead. Another twenty miles and we stopped again, this time on the hard surface, to listen to the loud clattering that had just developed apparently in the engine block. It was one of those noises that make you glad you don't have to pay personally for repairs. As there were only forty miles left to Port Augusta we decided to try inching the truck along under its

Top: Bush bashing. *Bottom:* The grader follows where the dozer has broken the trail.

own power and assist it on the rises with a few pounds of towing power from the Rover.

After ten miles of this it was my turn to stop to trace the cause of a pronounced missing in the Rover engine, which suddenly had lost half its effort. Two spark plugs were burnt right out, so we replaced them and continued for less than a mile before the missing occurred again. The same thing had happened. This time I noticed some water present, and to a bush mechanic like me that indicated a blown head gasket, but nevertheless I installed the last of our supply of plugs and we both crept our vehicles away from the scene. We wanted to try to reach Port Augusta where we could have meals and possibly negotiate with the railways. There, too, I planned to ask for help, on the radio transmitter installed in the vehicle, from the Woomera end. Very soon the engine trouble again developed but as the motor was still going I tried to ignore the noise, as did the other driver with his clattering one which was getting worse all the time.

We were supposed to be on our way to Central Australia and it began to dawn on me that, although we weren't complaining, we were having a slightly uncertain start. Both of us had experienced many such things before in the desert but that was well away from civilization where one expected them; not on a bitumen road within sight of the lights of towns.

Eventually we chugged into "the Port" with our two vehicles, one sounding like a cement mixer and the other a chaff-cutter, and positioned them by the kerb in a quiet street before daring to switch off the engines. After consulting the railways about sending the boring plant on to Woomera with them it was time to camp, so we lay in our swag rolls on the floor of the truck, under the machine, hoping we would not be arrested for not having a "fixed place of abode," as they say in the papers. Next morning, after using water from the tank on the vehicle for a shave and clean up, and having breakfast at a shop, we went to a garage to see what they could do for the Rover. I'd

Top: First cut through the virgin mulga. *Bottom:* Gunbarrel Highway — as straight as this.

already planned to have the truck taken back to Adelaide on one of our fleet of semi-trailers ferrying constantly back and forth with other equipment for the Range, and to attempt to tow the plant out to the job in the desert on a second truck we had stored at Woomera.

The mechanics at the garage soon discovered that my vehicle had come in on only the one cylinder after the other three plugs had gone. This news was followed by their discovery that a cracked cylinder head was the cause of it all. I could now string out my aerial in their shop to ask base for a replacement, as this would be quicker than waiting for the garage to have one sent. In the meantime, with the aid of a crane, the railways had transferred the boring plant from our sticken lorry to a goods truck and we had arranged the lorry's return on a semi. Then, as Bill and I were having dinner, someone came along on his way to Woomera and offered to take one of us ahead with him if that would help. I stayed behind; the driver went off to Woomera to look after the servicing of our second truck and to collect the plant from the railways at the siding when it arrived. It was now a week since we'd left Adelaide and we were still struggling to complete the first small stage of the trip in hand.

At last the day really did come when we were ready to leave Woomera, with the plant in tow behind the serviceable truck and the Land-Rover with its stock of spare parts replenished. The drilling team were to be flown up to us by the Air Force to operate the plant once we'd manoeuvred it into position at the site, but the date for this was deferred until further notice from us, and I went to farewell the Air Force Superintendent at Woomera before setting off. When he came over to watch our departure he casually remarked that he thought the boring rig could just about fit inside a Bristol Freigher aircraft if the wheels on the rig were removed. Almost too readily I agreed. I had been concerned for some time at our prospects of being able to tow such a weight over the sandhills; we had not yet made a road of any sort over the last several hundred miles of our journey. It was going to mean dragging the plant over the mulga-covered sand ridges by long cables attached to it after the truck itself had negotiated each ridge on its own. As there were hundreds of them it would take the two of us quite some time and effort.

So we were very pleased to arrange for the plant to be flown up to us after we had arrived and had advised over the radio when to let it come. We lost no time in uncoupling the draw bar from the truck and headed off without it, knowing that the "Super" would take care of all the details. I naïvely thought that the eventful but rather shaky start to this trip was all the bother we were going to have, but as it turned out our troubles were really only just beginning.

We covered the next three hundred miles so easily that I was reasonably sure everything was now all right. We would cover the remaining two hundred miles in a couple of days, radio for the plant to be flown in with the drillers and rations, and the future big scheme would be already under way. I was wrong!

Soon it was time to camp, and we cast a hungry eye over our scanty rations which we had meant to last us only until arrival of the plane. There was enough, that is, provided nothing went wrong, but we would have been happier to be carrying more and not relying so completely on outside help. As it was, the vehicles were loaded with drums of fuel, oxygen and acetylene bottles, and other necessary items. Anyway, at this stage there was no real cause for concern, and we lay down among the sandhills as a bank of ominous black clouds gathered overhead.

The sandhill crossings were made easier next day as there was a light mist of rain, which had started sometime during the night, and we came within an easy day's journey of our destination by nightfall. At last everything seemed straightforward. The next day we pushed off into the scrub, gloomy and dark after the rain in the bush, and were eagerly looking forward to the aeroplane's landing a day later with its supply of food, machinery, and operators. By the middle of the afternoon we were passing through the she-oaks growing from the travertine limestone outcrop, a forerunner of the actual claypan. Ahead lay steep, banked washaways and the last sand ridge bordering what was to be our home for most of the next two years.

The sandhill was completely covered with a thick mat of

bright purple parakeelya flowers, all rising up out of the carpet of yellow desert daisies and everlastings on the mulga flats, which had good rains during the growing season, something rare in these parts. It seemed almost a crime to be driving heavy vehicles over such a vivid "Garden of Eden." We roared up our engines for the last charge over the sandhill and when we reached the top the scene spread out before us was unbelievable. There, where we had planned our mile-long, iron-hard, flat, natural aerodrome, was the claypan, now looking more like an inland sea with the whole area completely under water, This immediately washed out our hopes and plans for an aircraft landing as surely as it had dissolved the "airport."

After skirting the shore to the spot we had previously selected for a camp, we immediately set up the radio aerial, cancelled our suggested E.T.A. (estimated time of arrival) for the landing, given the day before, and deferred all action at H.Q. until further notice. I remembered once being in an aeroplane that landed on a dry claypan and, while the stores were being unloaded, a sudden cloudburst had just moistened the surface. We had hurled off the load at a great rate to try for a take-off before the ground became too slippery. The pilot had run up his engines, and let off the brakes, only to have the plane slew round at right angles in the first ten yards as it slithered about in the mud. I realized how impossible it would be to land on such a frictionless surface and hope to stop before skidding headlong into the bush without the wheels even turning.

As soon as contact was made over the radio, and before I had a chance to relate the new turn of events, the base sent me the information that the plane was all loaded and ready for an immediate take-off. I felt quite a wet blanket as I replied with my message to cancel the flight. There was now nothing anyone could do but wait for it to dry out; apart from the ground crew who had to unload the aeroplane to release it for other duties and return the fresh rations to the stores. Bill and I tied up a canvas camp sheet to sleep under, for the black clouds made it almost dark hours before time, and we opened a tin of meat for tea. For once we weren't short of water, but we had to ration our food to make it last for an indefinite period, as already there was precious little left. We worked out that with one tin a day between us the meat would last for five days, and we could use honey in our mugs of tea instead of sugar. How we had come to place so much reliance on outside help I could not understand. We put some dry wood under the truck for the morning, and finally went to sleep. Fortunately we had a low stretcher each, which kept us out of the main stream of water and the waves. There was another downpour during the night, and the water was now deep enough to float our hobnailed boots away well out of reach by morning.

Next day we occupied ourselves putting up some tents and doing what Robinson Crusoe must have done in the early days of his adventure — making our area habitable. But of course we didn't need his fence. Things weren't so bad after we'd finished, and having a rifle each we went off in opposite directions to see if any of the rabbit warrens had been recently occupied. We met back at camp with nothing to show, so opened our tin of meat and had a drink of honey tea. Ugh!

Two tins later, no more rain having fallen, the claypan was much improved. After a fast drive down it in the Rover, a quick application of the brakes, and then a sharp turn, we decided it was nearly ready for a safe landing and radioed back to that effect. The voice from base sounded a little anxious about us, but assured us the plane would be loaded again the next day when the claypan would be quite safe. We thought that at last we could throw away the few magazines we knew from cover to cover as we would soon be living in the land of plenty. So far neither of us had sighted a rabbit or anything else to shoot, but that didn't matter now.

The next afternoon, when we called base to check on the E.T.A. and other things, the astounding news came back that the boring plant had broken its main axle while being towed to the aircraft for loading, the wheels had fallen off, and it was in the heavy equipment workshop undergoing a major repair job. We were bending over the speaker to hear the transmission through the static noises and when we heard the news looked at each other and burst out laughing.

It didn't worry us at all. The initial feelings of hunger had passed, as usual, and it now started to sound funny. These sort of things had never put us out, but we were grateful not to have a grouch in the camp with us.

The transmission went on to ask if we would like a small, faster aircraft to make a special flight to bring us out some food, but we replied that we would be all right for the days it would take to have the machine mended.

The ony thing it would mean to us was that we would have to make a more determined effort to lie in wait for rabbits and set out from camp earlier each day. These trips were made silently on foot, and our knuckles showed through more and more each day as we gripped our rifles. After the next trip we both had some luck and returned to camp each triumphantly holding up his kill. Bill had a good-sized rabbit — and a heavier bore rifle — but even what was left of his rabbit was larger than the one I was clutching as I struggled in. It would have been far too young even to attend rabbit kindergarten. At first Bill thought I'd shot a good-sized rat! We stirred up our fire, which was always warm, and, to use the term loosely, cooked them.

It seemed months since we'd left Adelaide and had run out of petrol in all that traffic. So much had happened to bring us to our present predicament, and civilization, which I suppose it was, seemed very far away. If we could have seen into the future, even from the time we had found the airstrip to be under water, we would have faced up to the not very pleasant thought of retracing our last few hundred miles through the scrub to fetch supplies, but as it was we were constantly being lulled into a sense of false security. Now we doubted our strength and ability to tackle such a trip.

Then one afternoon, after switching off the vehicle engine which we'd left running to recharge the battery for the radio, we knew everything was foolproof. The claypan was dry and hard, the sky was cloudless, the plane was reported loaded and ready for take-off once more (that ground crew must have thought this was all some kind of a joke), and we could expect the plane to reach us about mid-morning. What could possibly go wrong now? We shaved and went to our tents for the night, but we both lay awake for hours thinking of bread with melon and lemon jam, fruit, eggs, and salty bacon.

Our dreams were not yet to come true. Just after midnight, something must have awakened each of us at the same time, as we both appeared at the flaps of our tents. We knew straight away what had been the cause. Spots of rain were hitting at the canvas, and in ten minutes a storm like no other we'd ever seen was lashing our tents with its full fury, and water was flowing rapidly down the gentle slopes of the claypan edge in the direction of the lower surface of our "landing field." No discussion being of use just then, we weakly waved our equally weak torches at each other and withdrew. Under the blue, cloudless sky next morning, with the bright rising sun reflecting across the expanse of water, the scene looked very pretty indeed.

Back to the old faithful radio, but although we called until the battery was almost flat again we couldn't raise any reply, so we loaded up our signal pistol with a red for danger flare and waited in the middle of the lake on a box, with a good supply of flares. Eventually we heard the drone of the engine, followed closely by an actual sighting of the plane coming straight for our camp, the latitude and longitude of which I'd taken from the stars and transmitted long before. We discovered later that the plane's radio was locked on to another air radio frequency for constant contact in case of any mishap as this was in the nature of a pioneering flight. This explained why we couldn't get in touch with them on the way. All we could do now was to keep firing red flares across their path each time they made a low circuit. Some strength was needed to pull the trigger, so we were forced to use two weak fingers. The pilots at last got the message and turned once more for base, disappearing into the sky with all that bread and jam still aboard. We sat watching the plane until it was no more than a black speck, and then agreed that if things didn't improve soon, we'd have to try to make it out of there. We reasoned that if you don't eat anything you get all sorts of thing wrong with you in later life, but right then it was not later life we were terribly concerned with, as we headed again for our favourite rabbit warrens, rifles in hand. After we had again charged our battery and made contact, the operator at the base station mentioned that we must be getting rather peckish by now.

The heat of the sun aided by a slight breeze worked wonders, however, and the next day saw the surface restored. Whereupon we all arranged for the procedure to be repeated once more. The plane was in the air two mornings after its last try, and in due course we heard the familiar drone of its engines — but that was all. For some time we couldn't see the actual plane, and when at last we did, it was way off to the south, circling and circling round the maze of smaller claypans looking for our special one. This was our cue to light all the smoke generators and old tyre bonfires we had prepared for just such an emergency. Either these or one of the many green flares fired eventually attracted their attention and the machine grew in size until it was overhead. It made one circuit of the area before coming in for a perfect landing, using our smoky fires in lieu of a wind sock for wind direction, then taxied over to our camp and switched off.

We were waiting by the door as it opened, and we clambered aboard amid the greetings of the air crew. As we searched through the loading with our sunken eyes we found the boring plant there all right, lots of lengths of boring casing, and many bags of coke for its drill sharpening forge, but nothing else. The pilots and crew were as amazed as we were to realize that no rations of any kind were on board. They explained that they had grabbed the aircraft waiting on the tarmac in the dark that morning and headed off to us as soon as possible. It looked as if the unfortunate ground crew, having loaded and unloaded the heavy boxes so many times, had finally got tired of the whole business and forgotten about them altogether. What actually happened was that the crates had been stacked in the store and locked up, while the fresh rations had been returned for use and not replaced.

At this stage a crew member produced a banana and began to peel it. When my friend and I saw him, we whipped it out of his hand and before he knew it we were eating half each. He told us with tears in his eyes that there were plenty more up on the rack, along with some biscuits, so we ignored everyone until they had all gone.

Although we were tempted to return to civilization on the plane, after it had been unloaded, for a meal, such a flight was just as unattractive as waiting for a ration trip promised for the next day. The idea was now to have everything loaded into tubular cardboard storepedos and dropped by parachute from the bomb rack of a Lincoln, so that reliance need not be placed on our airport facilities any more. Sitting on the bags of coke we talked with the well-fed drilling team until the Bristol had disappeared beyond the trees on the mulga-covered skyline and told them all that had happened before their arrival. We hastened to explain, after noticing their expression, that the cracked head we got at Port Augusta really was on the vehicle engine.

This whole adventure was not dissimilar to many others we had experienced, when everthing seems to happen at once, although in between we had long, relatively trouble-free periods. It was an amazing phenomenon in the bush and we learnt to live with and accept it without question.

When the Lincoln flew over next morning and asked us over their radio, this time tuned in to us, just where we would like the food to be dropped, we replied that out in the middle of the smooth claypan would be wonderful, as it would be easier on our elbows and knees when we crawled out to fetch it.

5

Methods of Attack

At the speed a bulldozer travels pushing a bladeful of dirt, it took some time for the homestead to pass from sight on the morning we left. As we lumbered around a rocky outcrop we could at last, incredible though it was, concentrate on the job for which all this preparation had been made.

As I have to ease off course around sand ridges and salt lakes, and weave about missing the thickets of heavier scrub that resist penetration by a vehicle, the wheel tracks left after my recce trips are often quite winding. But I always try to return to a central axis, the direction of which I determine prior to setting out, so the tracks at least follow a consistent bearing. If a series of points were selected about two miles apart along the path of the track and joined by straight lines, a considerable ironing out would result, and this in effect is what we do. The bulldozer can achieve the straight line if started off in the right direction, and this is done in various ways according to the type of country and the intensity of growth.

After reaching a point on the tracks by Land-Rover, which seems, from a constant study of the built-in compass on the way, to be at a good average, I have to attract the attention of the bulldozer operator who is waiting on his machine at the head of the road. Unless obviously hopeless, I first try a sun flash from a mirror aimed at the spot from where the sound of the idling machine is coming, and then scan the area, which very often is only trees and scrub. To attain extra height, this is done from the roof of the vehicle, and usually within seconds, even though the normal line of sight is blocked by scrub, the throttling-up noise tells me the operator has seen the flash and is on his way. The powerful beam can usually pierce the minute breaks in the leaves and branches that obstruct vision. But if after half a minute of scanning there is still no sudden increase in the sound of his engine, I know that the beam cannot get through to him, so I fire the flare pistol, vertically into the air. This method never fails, but to save shots the mirror is always tried first.

When the signal has been received the operator observes which tree or bush appears on line, selecting one as far from him as possible, and, pulling the master clutch, drives straight at it with the blade of the bulldozer several feet off the ground. After the sighter has been run down, the resulting line can be carried on indefinitely if need be with the operator looking behind at the beaten path left by the dozer, instead of in front at the wall of mulga. On reaching me, he turns his machine, this time with the blade down, and cuts his way back along his own tracks, clearing away the debris. With a little practice these lines come out surprisingly near, if not right on, the spot I have indicated, and the heavier and thicker the scrub the more accurate, as the line is more defined.

To prevent overhanging branches ripping at canopies and brushing the sides of trucks on their future trips, we widen the cut line to almost double; this is done on the third trip of the dozer, with its blade angled, as it returns to me once more. Meanwhile I have had time to check ahead for the details of obstacles to be avoided, and sometimes I decide that the same line can be carried on again. In this case I wait for the return of the dozer and indicate the fact with a hand signal. If a bend is necessary, I set off just before the driver gets back and position myself at another point on the tracks, by which time he is ready and waiting for his next direction.

In open country neither mirror nor flare is usually necessary as the driver can see my black and white vehicle against most backgrounds at great distances and so can come direct to it. I can let him know when it is in place by opening the door wide, or, when the heat shimmer makes that sort of signal difficult, a single flick with the mirror starts him on his way. Another method is used when, after computing a bearing, and knowing there is nothing ahead in the way of obstruction but mulga, we make the road adhere to this bearing by standing behind the dozer with a prismatic compass, guiding its start-off and keeping it on line by hand signals. When the bulldozer is out of sight in the dust and haze, the driver can carry on the line as usual, going sufficiently far each time to enable him to arrive back by knock-off time, estimating the distance by his watch. A half-hour drive forward would mean three-quarters of an hour's bulldozer back, and so on.

On one of these occasions we carried the line on for eighty-three miles, and many straights of five, ten, and twenty miles were possible. A certain amount of criticism has been levelled against us for the monotony of our roads, and this might be justified. But the fact was always uppermost in my mind throughout the survey and construction that the straighter the road the shorter. I would arrive at the initial bearings from astronomical observations for latitude and longitude, which I would take on the recces as well as on the finished road at strategic points, and these gave me the most help.

Bends and sharp curves could come thick and fast without being the slightest burden on our consciences in the confused sandhill belts and around salt pans or rocks. Once I was forced to spiral my way out of a completely blocked-off sandy valley, and many violent A-bends appear where the road negotiates sand ridge fade-outs.

The grader follows the dozer, after it has completed its work, to put the finishing touches. As it cannot push through a path of its own, the operator is sometimes hard pressed in dense bush to find a turning area. Unlike the steel-tracked machine, its tyres will not stand up very well to mulga stakes; a grader is much more like an instrument than any of the other earth-moving plant.

Small branches, stumps, roots, and stones are always left behind the grader after its final cut along a new road in the bush. So along comes the handyman who is also the "cherry picker,'' a name given to one who cleans up such areas by hand. If the debris is not removed during the making of the road, it becomes a constant hazard to future traffic, causing staked tyres and damage to the under surface of any vehicle unlucky enough to have one tip as it passes over the object. This is an uninteresting though important job that must keep abreast of the overall progress.

As far as possible at the time, this is now a finished job and often has to remain untouched, except when the necessity arises and we have the time or the opportunity to cope with it. Being new, these roads are always ''heavy'' to drive on until traffic compacts them hard with normal usage. This is not an even process, and in order to save tremendous wear and tear on our own supply trucks, which have to travel over different sections on increasingly distant projects, we try to find the time to give the road extra brushes over with the grader only. This may not be done for several years, and depends on our availability and the location of subsequent road requirements.

The camp, then, comes last, moving along the newly made road as far as it can by noon, or to a space that we might have been forced to bulldoze out of the scrub for an overnight stop. We try to arrange the cuts so that we can have the machine back at this spot at the head of the road by lunch time, where the fitter can refuel and service it during our meal, preventing loss of time, and have it ready for us to carry on with immediately afterwards. Otherwise he has to come out to wherever it happens to be at midday. The grader is serviced during the day when it stops on its way past the camp, and it is in the camp overnight. The dozer is left as far along the road as we've been able to get it, and we return to camp at the end of each day over the road that has come into existence that afternoon.

As we continue on in the mornings, with the grader catching up, the others pack up and move camp once more to be in time to prepare dinner at the new site. In more open areas we leave it to them to drive on as far as they can along the previous afternoon's work and the new road of each morning, the farther they go the greater the saving of fuel used in travelling to and from camp. Although the members

61

develop a keen interest in the progress of the work, they are always ready for a small bucket shower and an early bed after tea at the end of each day.

If anything unforeseen happens to the routine, we have to cope with it in whatever way appears suitable at the time. Flat tyres on the grader are usually noticed by the cherry picker, who in the workshop Rover goes for the fitter and spares. The reasons for a signal to me by means of the dozer throttle could be, depending on what machine we had, a broken cable or fractured hydraulic line on the blade-lift mechanism, or perhaps undue boiling caused by the limit being reached in the amount of rubbish in the radiator core. But in proportion to the beating these machines take, it is truly remarkable how seldom they give trouble.

One disaster struck us so early in our work that I thought its recurrence would be frequent, judging by the routine nature of it. Actually it never happened again. The blade of the grader, which was buried under a mound of dirt spilling as usual from the extremity, came to a sudden and very definite stop upon encountering a submerged mulga root, the tree belonging to it having only been snapped off by the dozer at the surface. This in itself might have been all right had the rest of the heavy machine with its ponderous momentum not gone on without the blade. After picking himself up off the floor the operator found that the foot it had taken for his machine to come to rest had been enough to tear a large ball joint out of its shattered socket near the front and break off the four holding studs. The grader had been rendered useless in the space of a second. One look was enough for even the most unmechanically minded to realize this, as I did after I'd got the cherry picker's message that something seemed to be ''goin' on at the grader.'' Setting up camp on the spot for the indefinite period of interruption to follow, I thought of how we were only twenty-five miles out and of the millions of mulgas in front.

There was nothing else for it but to obtain new parts and repair the damage. The new parts would have to come from Alice Springs, more than two hundred miles away — a distance we were soon to consider as being closer than next door. Taking the broken parts and a list from the fitter, I set out immediately for the Alice, leaving the others to dismantle anything necessary to have the machine ready for the replacements. After driving all night, I stopped at five in the morning on the outskirts of the town, and fell asleep. Around midnight, during the trip, a pair of headlights approaching from the opposite direction grew in intensity for an hour and we both stopped as we drew level. The driver was the manager of the Alice Springs agency for our plant, and he gave me a letter of introduction to his staff asking them to give me all possible assistance. Coincidences such as this happen quite often in these parts. The sun woke me at eight, and putting on a shirt and socks I drove into the town to where my friend had directed. It was ten years since I had been in Alice Springs.

A frail gentle-looking woman came to the counter and I showed her the note, inquiring if there was anyone I could speak with regarding my requirements. Clasping her hands she said she might understand if I told her the trouble, and would possibly be able to handle the order herself. I hoped I didn't sound too doubtful as I described what had happened, making it the least technical and as simple as I could, while unwrapping from a sugar bag the shattered and distorted bits and pieces. When I had finished, she told me the serial number and horse-power of the particular machine the bits had come from, and said there were certain spring washers and shims missing from my collection which I would also need.

Apologetically she reached for a parts book from which to obtain the numbers, explaining that she often had difficulty in remembering the one attached to those special studs. Then she turned to a new arrival to say that she had discovered a flaw in a diesel injector of his and a replacement was on its way. Back to me she asked if the front surface, where the blind tapped holes that held the holding studs were located, had been damaged; if so, she said, I should borrow a plug tap. My jaw dropped, and I looked at her blankly, groping for words that would sound intelligent to her, as she carried on with her technical lecture. Without reference of any kind she mentioned they didn't have the socket in stock but that there was one in Sydney. She would signal for it immediately, and it would be here on the afternoon's plane.

Just then her help was needed with the sequence of installing a new cable in an overhead loader; she made the contractor happy by telling him she now had the new tine and shoe for his K30 ripper. I arranged to return in the afternoon, and I walked out feeling quite numb after hearing her explanation of how the double-ended threading on the studs she had in stock would fit our machine as long as she supplied the nuts and shims. The polite little woman then attended to a husky customer covered with dust, and her conversation about his fifty-yard scraper was still ringing in my ears as I drove away.

As I hadn't had anything to eat since lunch the day before, I felt I needed something now, the quiet, unassuming lady having made me feel weaker than ever. Noticing a large painted arrow pointing to a shop with a *CAFÉ* sign on it, I stopped and left Rover at the side of the street. I tried the door around the corner labelled *ENTRANCE*; it seemed a little stiff to open at first, but I put that down to my recent weakness, and pushed harder. Still it resisted, so I gave it a good bump with my shoulder. The whole thing came off its hinges with a rush and I fell flat on my face on top of the door. After disentangling myself from a curtain I got up and found I was in a bedroom. I breathed a sigh of relief that nobody was in the pink-covered bed.

My hunger gone by now, I left promptly and hurried to my Rover for a quick getaway. As I raced round the corner I rechecked the café sign, and saw an attempt had been made to obliterate it with watery whitewash. Reaching the Land-Rover I noticed a pair of boots sticking our from underneath it. Turning whiter than the sign, I tried to remember whether I had felt a bump as I pulled up. Shakily I knelt down, preparing myself for the gory sight I was sure I was about to see, when a voice drawled out, "Good day." An old bushman had been studying the construction of the sump protection plates I had added in Adelaide, and he now

Len Beadell and Mount Beadell.

asked for more details. He had thought, from the general appearance of the vehicle, that it was meant for bush work, and out in this kind of country we are all interested in each other's ideas on modifications for cross-country work. There was no one about so he just lay down under it to see for himself. There followed a long conference during which I asked him about the café — it appeared it hadn't been used for years.

I left him sitting on the footpath rolling with laughter at what had happened, and drove off to wait in the bush where I was safe. When it was time for me to collect the spares I ventured back into town and there, waiting for me, were my socket and extras all the way from Sydney; and there, too, before allowing me to go, the little lady explained to me how to use them all. Being used to her by now I didn't worry so much when she admonished a rugged character twice her size for not servicing his double drum sheep's foot roller.

By the time I arrived back at my camp after another all-night drive I was feeling even more hungry, but it was easier to cope with there than in those big city cafés. Everything had been made ready to install the new parts, an we went on with the road after only one day's delay, the grader catching up with the progress later.

The November temperatures, averaging one hundred and five degrees, persuaded us to arrange for a steel awning for the open dozer in the new year. The operator fried in the sun each day and it was almost impossible to touch the controls and the seat. The rate of progress was a fairly constant four to five miles a day and I could rely on at least a hundred miles of new road in each working month, which proved a good average throughout the project. As the country altered we could do up to seven miles on some days in the open. Here we would bulldoze forward as we went, without returning, and the grader would handle the widening. I was consequently much more pressed to keep up in these areas.

About this time discussions were going on at H.Q. about the need for establishing a suitably situated weather recor-

Top: Bogged . . . *Bottom:* . . . and bogged again.

ding station, in an area more than three hundred miles distant. A satisfactory geographical location, roughly in the centre of a complete void, had been decided on from information supplied by existing meteorological stations around Australia. As well as providing a valuable and permanent contribution to the recording of our overall weather patterns, reports from this area by our department were necessary for a current series of trials. To enable such an outpost to be established was the prime reason for this first half of the road across the Centre, and subsequent projects, although of the utmost importance later on, were incidental to this initial one.

Plans were being made for a combined party to visit the locality suggested, with a view to actually pin-pointing a site which met the technical requirements of the Bureau of Meteorology, fulfilled our needs, and satisfied geological conditions indicating the proximity of water to be had by drilling. Aboriginal ceremonial grounds, which are situated throughout the bush with no visible indication, had also to be considered, as they must be respected and if possible not in any way violated. The expedition was planned to be roughly concurrent with the completion of our first hundred miles of road, and as it was almost Christmas I was not particularly looking forward to it. If the temperatures now were almost unbearable, they would be worse then, but it was necessary to decide on a site before the new year, to allow me to carry on with the road without delay.

So we crashed on through the scrub, the cook battling with the ever increasing hordes of flies, which were enough to test the endurance I could expect from the party later on. I often thought that if these men came back with me after Christmas they would be good men. Two nights in the one camp, such as at the week-ends when we had a "spell" on Sundays, did not just double the number of flies encountered in one night's stay; their increase was astronomical. We were constantly thirsty, and water didn't seem to relieve our craving; the dry dust billowing up around the plant clung to our sweating bodies so that our tongues, teeth, and eyes were our only noticable features. Trying to fill in the Sunday "day off" under these conditions was torture, and we were all glad when Monday came and we could get on with the job. We'd just sit, in a pool of trickling sweat, beating at flies or trying to move out of the direct rays of the sun. But my newly formed party proved their endurance, and their reaction to this kind of pressure, by coming back with me in the new year.

The big diesel engine of a bulldozer is started by means of a small petrol pilot motor coupled to it with a pinion cog and clutch. When the big motor fires it is supposed to throw out the pinion automatically, as is the case with any starter on a car. But if the little cog remains locked in the big ring gear after the diesel engine starts spinning, then the pilot motor becomes driven at an impossible rate; after eighty miles of road had been laid down, we discovered what finally happens in such a case. We had started the pilot motor in the morning, and engaged the pinion and clutch, waiting for the oil pressure to build up before closing the decompression lever and opening the throttle for fuel to cause the big motor to fire.

Everything sounded all right until the big engine started, but before we realized what was happening the little one began spinning at a supersonic rate, flying to pieces as we dived for the protection of the steel tracks. The pinion had jammed in the ring gear. At least the dozer was now ready for use, and we could carry on as long as the diesel kept going. With this in mind, the operator was more than careful to prevent throttling down too low and causing it to stall, and we carried on as usual until lunch time. Leaving it at a fast idle we told the fitter the sad news, and he asked how far we had to go. I had worked it out that three days would see us through this year's work as far as the dozer was concerned. It seemed that a towing start was possible provided the heavy machine was left in a place with a good open area in front so the grader could manoeuvre. This was the only machine we had capable of moving the dozer, so by doing this each morning and leaving the engine running all day we were able to complete the first stage of our project.

Arriving at the Happy Family's area in a cloud of dust

I thought of the turkey's nest dam and, as we looked about for a tree with a strong enough branch to use as a crane, I knew we didn't have the best equipment in the north-west after all. The first thing to do was to place the crippled bulldozer under the tree, with the pilot motor positioned where it could be lifted out by a chain hoist tied to the branch, and only then could we shut off the diesel for the last time that year. The next few days were occupied with the removal of the injured motor and much mechanical work on the other vehicles. "The Family" didn't fail to live up to my earlier impressions, and we all had a pleasant time, singing cowboy songs at night after the day's work. In an effort to add variety to the repertoire the men made jokes about how the chaff was trickling out of the guitar, but it was of no use — the cowboy songs kept coming.

Hearing over the transmitter that an air reconnaissance had also been organized to take place immediately prior to the ground expedition, I arranged to have our party return south on the same plane as the pilot motor when we had finished with it, leaving the trucks and plant in the bush over Christmas. The aircraft was to land on an almost natural airfield where we had arranged to have a load of petrol waiting, carted there by the "punctual" mail driver. Three more Land-Rovers straight from the workshops had been brought up overland by now, all in good condition, which was just as well, since mine, as usual at this time of the year, was suffering horribly from its annual bout of bush bashing.

In due course the plane came into view and landed in the heat haze rising from the airfield. The other members of our expedition alighted, and I'm certain experienced their first qualms concerning the wisdom of agreeing to such a trip in December.

6

A Christmas Expedition

The aeroplane we had for the job was one that needed petrol to make it go. It was astonishing how quickly it took on the appearance of a neat pile of scrap metal when it came to the night before the reconnaissance flight and the mail truck had not arrived with the petrol for it. The plane had been able to carry only enough fuel for the trip to the airfield and back, so the success of the survey flight now depended completely on the local mailman.

After dark we sat around wondering what had gone wrong with his truck, which I knew to be composed of more number eight fencing wire than the original vehicle. It had no doors or windscreen, and the mudguards were made from oil drums held together by wires joined over the top of the engine, a huge diesel, which, as there were no side plates, was in full view, and the enormous radiator was protected by the six-inch bore casing bumper bar. Still, I had quite a respect for it; it had kept us supplied with fuel for our last hundred miles of road making. But now I began to wonder, as did the others. We had been very definite, when we first asked him to do the job, about when the flight was to take place, and that it was most important for petrol to be delivered to the airfield on time.

It was now decided that the aircraft would have to return in the morning, using what fuel it had left, and we would carry on overland. I felt the flight could have helped me in the following year's work, but at the same time, especially in the heat of summer, I remembered I was not a very good airman. It was, nevertheless, a disappointed lot of men who lay down to sleep after loading our old bulldozer's pilot motor and the personal belongings of my party for the return trip.

Before dawn next morning a faint sound penetrated our subconscious, and woke us; once awake we couldn't think what had caused it. Some minutes later we heard a more definite sound and our pilots wondered who could be flying another search plane so soon. Just then, in the first light of dawn, someone noticed a small spiral of dust, and into binocular view chugged a huge load of petrol drums, with the mail truck underneath.

Our great silver aircraft immediately lost its scrap-heap appearance — we had never really thought it looked ugly anyway. As the old diesel shuddered to a stop without the use of brakes, the mailman informed us he'd been bogged in the sand and had been forced to leave his trailer with the rest of the petrol. But everything was all right because an old aboriginal driver was coming along in an escort vehicle and they would go for it as soon as they'd unloaded. I took the party on a tour of inspection of the truck, and they wondered what magic kept it going — even without a load and trailer. We were up to the wire and bore casing when the mailman apologetically pointed out that it didn't look much, "but she's a good old bus." He added, in case they'd missed the fact, that lately it seemed to be falling to bits.

A motor-driven pump was already at work pumping the petrol into the plane, so that, together with what there was for the return trip, we now had sufficient for the survey. The party's ultimate journey back to civilization thus depended on the subsequent salvaging of the sand-bogged trailer, but after this episode they had confidence that in due course it would arrive, The aboriginal escort then came into sight, carrying out his duties to the bitter end, and without a word began checking over his vehicle. Our conversation was periodically interrupted while time out was taken to read the sums on the tyre gauge he held up for inspection; the old native would resume his pumping if the stick wasn't out far enough.

By the time all was ready for the take-off, the sun was out in all its force and the aluminium plane was like an oven. I already felt off colour as we climbed aboard, only to sit wringing wet for half an hour until something was attended to in the cockpit. After take-off I went up to the front in order to have a better vantage point, and secured the navigator's map. What seemed like hours later, but was really much less, there slowly took shape on the northern skyline a hazy blue line of hills — the Rawlinson Range, and our destination. I began to wish the mail truck had stayed bogged; I was not feeling at all steady, and my heart dropped as I thought we must be much closer. The pilot was a rather large man and beads of perspiration were rolling from his face, so I made sure I concentrated only on the map and the country. He was in high spirits, of course, because the mission was once more under way, but I'm afraid I couldn't share his elation.

Flying low for a better study of the ground, the plane was thrown about by the heat thermals and air pockets until we reached the Rawlinsons, where I gritted my teeth and tried to take more of an interest. I had to keep thinking of our future ground work. On the way I had identified a natural pass through a bad bottleneck of sandhills and rocky mountain ranges, so I made a special note of it on the map. This was the only obvious way through a difficult section halfway up, and I knew that wherever else the road went I would put it through here. It proved to be an extremely valuable piece of information and well worth the whole effort, but that was the only help the flight gave me.

After a closer look at the proposed site, involving circling and banking, shuddering and surging up and down, an extensive examination of the Rawlinson Range from the air was made probably for first time in history. Then, as the pilot mopped his face and neck, he asked me what I'd like to see next to help in our future work. My first thought was, "Are you kidding?" as I secured the navigator's protractor and read off a straight line bearing to the airfield. I informed him that this course would help me most in the work to come as it might keep me alive long enough to do it.

Not wishing to appear distrustful, and before giving way to delirium, I glanced furtively at the compass to ensure it read the homeward bearing. We must have landed back at the airfield because as the doors were being opened I was out of that machine before the catches were in place. I'm not sure what happened in the next hour or so, but the trailer had apparently arrived because the plane was being refuelled, and the rest of my party said something about seeing me later. I very much doubted if I'd ever see anyone again, as the large pilot once again had the plane in the air. He must have had the stamina of an ox, for I couldn't have lived through another flight. It took me four days to recover as it was.

At last there seemed nothing more to hold us up, so we set off with our four Land-Rovers and six men. Usually I like to look over the straight-line course first, and put in the deviations later if that proves impracticable, and as I felt I could use this trip for the additional purpose of the future road recce everyone was only too agreeable to follow along.

All went reasonably well for the first day, although I'd already decided a considerably more detailed survey would be necessary later owing to the rocky nature of the country. The Rovers' radiators were heating to a varying degree depending on their position in the line, the first collecting most of the spinifex husks, the second some of what were left, and so on. Mine was already in a bad way before starting, even though we had first blown out the core with our truck compressor, but as it took in the bulk of the husks it was now boiling furiously in spite of the protecting screens. That night one of the members helped by hooking out the rubbish with a length of soft copper wire, as no compressor was available.

Everyone was glad to be under way at last after all the preparations, and we were still able to laugh and joke at this stage. Thinking of the various competitions for "Miss Australia" and "Miss Orange Blossom Festival," I often thought I should have a "Mr Expedition" ribbon made, which could be presented to the one who remained the most jolly throughout. The winner would have to have greeted everyone in the party cheerfully every morning, and never have become visibly upset under stress.

Nobody had to be reminded that water was as precious as liquid gold in these areas, after someone timidly mentioned a moist rag wash.

Next day we reached a hopelessly confused belt of sandhills surrounding a rocky jump up named Mt Gosse after the man who first visited and named Ayers Rock. Engines were revved to screaming pitch to negotiate the saddles in the sandhills, and they boiled and spluttered in soaring temperatures of a hundred and twenty degrees, as we travelled on tyres deflated to their limit. I was just thinking that here was one area definitely to be avoided when someone who was under a vehicle digging it out of a hummock called out that according to the air photos this was a sandy area. We couldn't help agreeing with the photos.

Soon my Rover stopped, and refused to go even after the "atomizer" treatment. This involved squirting a small mouthful of water over strategic petrol lines in order to relieve a vapour lock when the engine would not respond to the starter; I found this would usually clear it. But now evidently something else was in trouble. It had stopped in an open area, half-way up a steep sand ridge, where the sun was unbearable and the metal parts were quite impossible to touch, even without the red-hot exhaust pipe adding to the Fahrenheit. I found the spark plugs had been cooked as black as coal but they appeared to be still working, and after searching for several hours, the trouble was located in the condenser. It resembled a knocked over honey jar with something like melted wax coming from its end; the engine fired at last when the condenser was replaced with a spare, allowing us to have a second run at the sandhill and carry on.

Even now I was just as pleased not to have had the benefit of air support as we did on a previous expedition, which incidentally resulted in the selection of the testing ground now known as Maralinga. On that trip, an aeroplane had been made available to us to drop supplies of fresh food, mail, petrol, and water periodically to our various camps among the sandhills. They would come down in the form of "storepedos"— cardboard cylinders with supply parachutes attached — all except the mail, which came down on a free fall.

One day we had summoned the plane to our transmitted latitude and longitude position in the difficult endless horizon of sandhill country for the purpose of dropping some necessary supplies. Talking to the air-crew by means of the radio as the plane circled overhead, we were delighted to hear that they had thought to collect some mail for us before taking off, and would make a low run to drop it out. Sure enough, as the plane came towards us at little over sandhill height, a small container with a length of white rag tied to it emerged from the cockpit and spiralled down into the scrub. It fell a hundred yards away, and as we picked it up we found the letters were rolled into a spent signal-flare cartridge-case with the rag tied through holes cut in the cardboard. I untied the white streamer and withdrew what turned out to be a single letter for me, which I opened, thinking of the marvels of modern civilization, and of what an efficient postman we had. It was certainly an unusual way to receive mail in such a wilderness of desolate isolation. My elation, however, was shortlived. I unfolded the cold informal page and read in large, stark, and black lettering, words as inhospitable as the surrounding country:

FINAL NOTICE
TAXATION DEPARTMENT

It appears that for some reason I had not received their other letters — possibly the last three postmen had perished — and that I owed them the balance of seven shillings and fourpence from my last return. It brought home to me clearly that "crime doesn't pay," and that you just can't escape from the long arm of the law. I had visions of being thrown straight into a debtors' prison, if I survived my present surroundings, to rot miserably on bread and water, which was at least more than I had here.

When I did eventually return to civilization, I took the letter, complete with the cartridge case and rag, into the deputy commissioner who had signed it, put them all on his polished desk, and told him the story. I found he was quite human after all.

Dark came upon us mercifully once more, and the expert with the copper wire again operated on the radiator, as everyone else had flat tyres to mend and vehicle wounds to lick. We were making an impression on the distance now, as seen from the "morale astrofix" I observed.

In due course, the Rawlisons could be seen occasionally from the top of a sandhill. There was much room for improvement in the straight-line course I had been trying, but this could not be known until it had been investigated.

I would have to find the ''pass'' later, perhaps on the return journey. As I had been using up everyone's spare condensers, they were becoming a little scarce, but luckily the last one held out. I once tried letting out some of the bottled-up hot air from around the engine by removing the bonnet cover. This quickly proved hazardous when the flying sticks, which collected in the enclosure like a crow's nest, caught fire. At the sight of flames appearing from the engine in my line of vision, I was roused into swifter action than I felt like and, with no water to spare, shovelled sand over the whole thing at a great rate, as the distributor cap already resembled a quartpot billy can on a cooking fire. Grateful that the wiring had not been burnt beyond repair, I replaced the bonnet immediately and resigned myself once more to vapour locks.

As it happened, we followed the range too closely when it was eventually reached, and the drivers did an excellent job negotiating the steep rocky gutters coming from it. They were all still in the running for the Mr Expedition ribbon, and that helped considerably.

I had been aware of a small trickle of water coming from the water pump for some time and it was becoming more of a flow at each stop, the radiator requiring an increasing quantity of water which we could barely afford. When I mentioned it that night as we mended our flat tyres, it settled the topic of conversation for the evening. It was impossible to return with our limited water supply and the heat as it was, unless something could be done. The native welfare member of the expedition came to light with a seal he had carried for a long time together with an impeller, which looked as if they belonged inside a water pump.

An impeller is a cast-iron wheel with fins attached for spinning the water and sending it on its cooling mission around the engine block. It seemed that a hydraulic press was needed to install these pieces, always provided the worn-out pump could first be taken apart. Placing the Rover in a dry creek bed alongside a large tree with a low fork in its trunk, the unusual operation to restore a water pump in the bush was attempted. There was nothing to be lost if it proved a failure, as the vehicle could not be driven back anyway, but on the other hand it just might work. I made a mental note that from now on a complete water pump would forever be part of my equipment.

This was going to take days, so the rest of the party went exploring on foot and noticed some small birds that kept to the one area. The geologist announced that he was about to perform his first offical duties as hydrologist for the party by discovering water. He dug a hole in a depression of the dry creek bed frequented by the birds and it soon became moist; then some actual water seeped into the bottom. After that each took turns at enlarging the hole until basinfuls of water were being thrown around with careless abandon. Tins were filled and, even though the water was brackish, our little expedition took on an altogether brighter complexion. This was the same creek bed in which Giles, more than eighty years earlier, had watered his twenty horses from what he had described as being a half-mile long lake.

Meanwhile I had unscrewed the unserviceable pump and dismantled it as far as possible. It was obvious the old impeller was holding back the offending seal inside and was there to stay, having been forced in the factory on to the shaft by tons of effort from a press. On examining the new impeller I saw that the hole for the shaft was machined through a thick collar of cast iron, as thick as the length of a small drill I had among my tools. There was nothing else for it but to sit in the sand and start drilling holes in the collar in an effort to break it away from the shaft. I sat there with the little hand-drill for nearly two days, being very careful not to break the only drill in the camp, and by then I had six holes through the thick collar across its diameter. It now remained to try a chisel and hammer in the hope that all this effort would finally break away the collar. Quite a lot depended on my success, and as the tension built up no one could watch the climax. Placing the chisel along the line of holes, I tried a tentative tap with the hammer; to my delight that was all it needed. The old impeller fell apart revealing through the rust the worn-out seal.

A hydraulic press was now needed, and this is where the fork in the tree came into the proceedings. Laying the water pump shaft on the ground alongside a seven-ton jack, which we always carry with us, with the new impeller covering the vital seal now in place alongside the shaft, and a ball hammer alongside the impeller to concentrate the pressure in the right spot at the collar, the overall length could be measured. This was marked in pencil in the tree fork, and with the razor sharp survey axe I managed to chop out my press. There was just enough lettering left on the jack to inform its user that when it was to be operated in a horizontal position the arrow had to be pointing upwards. Silently thanking the makers for their foresight, I set up all this apparatus in the press, checking the straight line of the axis with a stretched-out length of grass.

Now came the final test of applying the strain with the jack to see whether the days of effort were to give any results. Once again everyone deserted the scene as they admitted they just couldn't bear to watch, but, to my relief, with every action of the jack the new impeller began to slide into place on the shaft. The strain must have been terrific on the tree as well as on me, but we both survived and soon the water pump was as new. Eight large official departmental envelopes, cut with care and oiled, served as the gasket to reinstall the unit on to the engine, and we were mobile once again. This pump was to last for the drive back not only to civilization but right to our workshops in Adelaide, where some unfortunate mechanic would be confronted with the puzzle of his career.

The pinpointing of the meteorological station could now continue with renewed supplies of water, and morale at a high level. A hard flat-topped rise became an obvious, unanimous choice for all concerned, only four miles from our Forked Tree Service Station where repairs are carried out while you wait, if you bring your own bed. The Rawlinsons would not obstruct low-flying weather balloons in windy flights, the prospect was good for the future boring programme to supply the site with water, and the interests of the natives were satisfied.

We camped on the site that night, and three stones were placed one on top of another to mark the birth of the Giles Meteorological Station, appropriately named after the first white man to have been in the area. These three small stones were an insignificant start to what now appears on all new maps of Australia, and is to be seen daily on our television screens in its place among the weather information charts.

But we still had to get ourselves out of these temperatures of a hundred and twenty, and cover the hundred and fifty miles back through the bush over a different route. Knowing that a star position would be needed for the report to the bureau, and a latitude and longitude would also help me in the new year, I set about observing the stars and finished the calculations before lying down for the night.

We set off next morning with doubts about ever being home in time for Christmas, now only a week away. On this part of the trip I discarded the straight-line route completely in favour of the "pass," using the return trip to try to locate it. The replenished water tins kept up with the boiling of the radiators caused by the husks, but the water pump on my vehicle held out and helped to conserve our supplies. Thick scrub in places and spinifex kept the pace down to almost a walking speed, and flat tyres came one after the other. A constant thought was that the last spare condenser was already in use, so we tried to keep down the heat of our engine by frequent stops to replace the water that had boiled away. The expert also made greater use of his bent copper wire husk remover.

The same lion-shaped mountain first seen from the air, which I knew to be an indication of the pass, gradually became visible from sand and stone rises, so we made for it feeling very pleased at our progress. But just as we reached it and found it to be up to all our expectations, the rear axle on my vehicle snapped, causing our newfound elation to be short-lived. With the tyres deflated even more than usual, the front wheels managed to pull the vehicle along for a few more miles until a fresh belt of sandhills began and it became obvious it would be impossible to continue. Now we were through the pass and more than halfway back, so we decided to rob another vehicle of its axle and leave it in the bush for recovery by our road party when we reached this area later with the construction. Two of the remaining three vehicles had only one driver each, and so the occupants of the robbed Rover split up and travelled in those.

The broken stub from the axle had become jammed in the differential, and its removal presented a further problem. This was solved by using a leg from a billy tripod and a jack handle. The leg was heated in a fire, which greatly helped to raise the normal day temperature, and hammered into a flattish, curved shape on a bumper bar. It was then hacksawed off a fraction longer than the jack handle which, being tubular, was slipped over it. When this prehistoric "instrument" was in place in the axle housing against the broken stub, and the opposite good one removed, a sharp blow with a heavy hammer was enough to dislodge the stub, firing it out of the other side like a rifle bullet. The jack handle had supported the thin, billy tripod leg in practice as well as in theory. A nasty accident was narrowly averted when someone, who was about to bend down to look in the opposite side to see how it was going, had his attention diverted a second before the steel flew past his legs. Mechanics do have other less exciting ways of coping with these situations, but we weren't feeling our brightest just then.

As we rushed on, leaving the Rover to the tender mercies of the bush but hoping to find it again some day, I somehow felt guilty of robbing a vehicle that would have been perfectly capable of making the journey back. Unfortunately, my Rover needed an overhaul for the new year's work, and carried instruments still wanted on this trip. A good opening for a speech to the transport officer at headquarters would be, I thought, a casual, "Oh, there you are. Now there's something we feel you should know . . ."

It took only a day to reach the airfield, where another plane had been organized to land and take the party away. I made a wide circuit of the aircraft, trying not even to look at it as the others eagerly climbed aboard. I'm sure they were all thinking the same as I was: that it would be a long time before they would again be members of a Christmas expedition in Central Australia. Although it would be difficult to judge with such a good group, I mentally pinned the Mr Expedition ribbon on the hydrologist.

Not long afterwards I learnt, with great regret, that our

expert with the bent copper wire had been killed in a traffic accident. I always think of him every time I clean husks from radiator cores.

Even before the plane had taken off, the native affairs member and I had started our thousand-mile overland drive south, where we arrived after all just in time for Christmas. I tried not to think about making a road to the three stones through the country we had just penetrated.

As I handed my Rover in to the workshops in Adelaide, I mentioned to the mechanics that there were a few things that probably needed looking into, including the water pump.

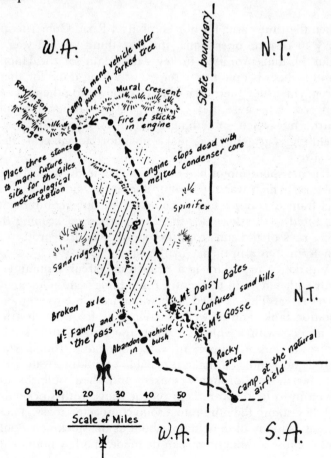

7

On the Road to the G-Isles

When the time came for our Gunbarrel Road Construction Party to resume operations, the first thing we did was to make the long-promised turkey's nest dam for the Happy Family. Bush people never regard anything done for them as repayment for their own kindness shown to others. They help people because they want to, without thought of any return, but when something is done for them are overwhelmingly grateful and make no effort to conceal their pleasure.

The new pilot-motor had been installed in the grown-over bulldozer which was roused into life again and serviced. A steel-framed canopy had been made to our requirements and fitted to the dozer for the dual purpose of keeping the direct rays of the sun from the operator and of protecting him from flying branches in the scrub.

A turkey's nest dam is a heaped-up circular mound of earth with a hole in the centre resembling a miniature volcano crater. This is filled with water from the overflow of a station tank, and as well as saving the frequent shutting off needed with a windmill when the tank is full, it also ensures a constant supply of water to a cattle trough when there is no wind. To make it capable of holding water, the loose earth is thoroughly soaked and then bullocks are driven in to it; they are kept on the move with stockwhips and they stamp the mud into a solid compacted mass. There are not as many of these dams about as the stockmen would like, because although one can be made in a few hours with

82

a bulldozer, it takes weeks using a horse and scoop.

Feeling better for having been able to help our friends, we once again left the homestead, driving off in a cloud of dust, and knowing that there would be no more signs of life until we reached an aboriginal mission in Western Australia — four hundred miles away.

Previous expeditions had brought me into contact with the next hundred and eighty miles of range country, and I knew that this would be our most pleasent section; in fact, it proved to be the most picturesque of the entire project. My old wheeltracks were being used currently by the members of a geological camp near the natural airfield from which we had set off on our recent air and ground survey trip.

Except when we were making the occasional dry creek crossing negotiable by vehicles and avoiding rock outcrops connected to the ranges, we covered this section at a fast clip. Spinifex-covered rocky ranges were always in view, and groves of black oaks added to the variety of the scenery, which helped to keep our minds off the heat and flies. We had resumed work early in the new year and still had at least three months of soaring temperatures ahead, before the flies disappeared on the eighteenth of May. On other projects, I had been connected with teams of British scientists who had kept asking "Look here, when do the flies go?" My answer was always, "The eighteenth of May." I made myself scarce on the nineteenth.

Although there were small patches of thick mulga scrub, most of the ground as far as the border into Western Australia was open spinifex. Beginning in the Northern Territory we moved into South Australia until we were ten miles south of the corner where the three State boundaries meet. To make the road more interesting we wanted to take it past this corner, but, after locating its approximate position astronomically, we found it to be in a very rocky area unsuitable for road making.

Everything was going well along this stretch until a signal flare I had shot for direction set fire to a particularly large area of spinifex. This frequently happened and the resulting fire usually burnt itself out very quickly. This night, however, we camped in an area where the fire could be seen, with its volumes of black smoke, in all directions. To see sheets of flame all around was disturbing, but I thought the fire wouldn't get past the ranges to the north, and it could go south for three hundred miles without doing any real damage. Westwards there was nothing to worry about for seven hundred miles, but the Happy Family lived only a hundred miles east. After I had explained these facts to the camp, in an effort to reassure myself that we weren't going to destroy Australia by fire, the cook summed up everyone's thoughts by saying, "Well, I'm glad I didn't start it, anyway." It was not at all in evidence next day much to my relief, and even though we were in the back country it made us more conscious of this during the rest of our work.

Another evening, when we were sitting under our canvas tent-like awning, an amazing thing happened. Everything was calm and still, without even the sound of the flies to disturb us as we ate our tea, when suddenly and without warning the tent took off like a rocket and swept everything off our little table. We came to our senses wondering what on earth had happened, until it dawned on us the handyman was missing. He often went round checking the dingo traps he always put out about this time, but on this night, because the traps were so far out, he had gone in the Land-Rover. We were camped on a stony place where the steel pegs couldn't be driven in easily, and for convenience the ropes had been tied to the workshop Rover. The handyman had forgotten this and, on finishing his tea, had driven off — taking the tent with him. It was obvious that even then he didn't know, and we stood by helplessly as our dining-room was carried along the dusty new road and out of sight. Fortunately it was a lovely night for eating in the open.

Another time the handyman was asked to fetch a drum of oil from a dump thirty miles back. When he hadn't returned after three days we decided to look for him, but on the night before we were to set out he drove into camp with the Rover smelling like a mobile candy factory.

He explained that the radiator was full of grape-fruit juice but that everything was in order. We had carried two cases of grape-fruit juice for two months, but as it was a little sour for our tastes we had thrown them off at the dump. When the handyman had gone for the oil the vehicle has started to boil becuse of a slipping fan belt, the water in the radiator had boiled away, and he had then used all his tank water. So, retrieving the two cases from the dump, he used the juice tin by tin and, by this ingenious method, got back to camp. The spashing of it on the fan belt had stopped the slipping, so we thought maybe he'd invented something.

We approached the area of the airfield after completing a total of two hundred and seventy miles of new road, and with only six hundred and thirty miles to go. The geological party were very pleased to see us.

Now came the dual task of making the road to the weather station site, marked only by three lonely stones, and of recovering the stranded Land-Rover from the sandhills. We had brought with us the necessary replacement axles and oils for the job but first we had to locate it again. It was about sixty miles away in a small local maze of sandhills and thick bush, but I thought that by following our own wheeltracks its rediscovery would be easy. So, while the rest of the camp stayed at the airfield to service the equipment in readiness for the next stage, the bulldozer driver and I went off to find the stricken Rover.

That night as we struggled back to camp, minus the Land-Rover, after nearly a hundred and fifty miles of travelling through bush and spinifex, and over sandhills, we had some explaining to do. The wind had completely blown the old wheeltracks away and without them it had been like looking for a needle in a haystack. As I was the only one who had been there before, I had tried to remember the pattern of the maze in the immediate vicinity, but each dune we crossed seemed the same. I began to feel sorry for the transport officer again, and thought that here was something else he should know. The next day I decided to change my tactics by making a wide circuit of the area, cutting the tracks where I knew them to be as they emerged from the pass, and attempting to follow them in from the opposite direction. In this way we found them as good as new and, following them in many instances by walking ahead when the dunes were reached, we found the Rover.

It was just as we had left it months before — still resting on mulga blocks, wheels inside the cabin out of the weather, and a box of eggs on the bonnet. I remembered that the eggs had been a little shaken by the end of the survey and were left behind. An anxious examination under the windscreen wiper revealed no parking stickers, so we set to work and soon had the vehicle back on its four wheels. Then came the operation of checking the engine and starting it with a spare battery brought for the job. This meant moving the eggs in order to lift the bonnet, but as soon as they were disturbed there was a series of minor explosions. Wondering how eggs look after months in that sort of heat, I had my face in an appropriate position over them when the first one blew up, setting off chain reaction. Apparently, when left for long periods in the sun, the original contents decompose to gases which under pressure convert the eggs into bombs requiring extreme care in handling, but all this didn't occur to me until they had converted me into something of an outcast for the rest of the day.

After the previous day's refresher course regarding the layout of the maze we had no difficulty in driving out of it, and headed triumphantly back to camp, this time with our two vehicles. The paper-work at the transport office could at last be straightened out.

We had been advised that the road to Giles would have to be capable of handling large semi-trailers carrying tons of building material. This information governed many decisions as to the size of the possible sandhill crossings, and the general course of the road would depend on these. Although the weather was still quite hot, it lacked the fierceness we had experienced in the same area during the Christmas expedition, and while the preparations were being completed for the next onslaught, I decided to repeat the trip alone.

This time I had the advantage of some knowledge of the country — I knew where not to put the road, and one place, through the pass, where it must go. This recce trip would govern the final route we would take, but each day throughout the construction the details would have to be studied.

The survey trip had gone so well as far as the pass that

I decided to push on at least to within sight of the Rawlinsons again. The scrub north of the pass had certainly not become any lighter than we had found it on our combined trip, and I had just as many flat tyres to mend as before. This scrub gave way to spinifex and long sand ridges that constantly eased me off the course I had worked out, but I had anticipated this from what little I remembered of my aerial view of the section. Here the ridges helped a little, in spite of the easing, being almost at right angles to the ones in the centre. At a suitable spot, and with the Rawlinsons in view, I decided to turn around and retrace my new wheeltracks back to camp, leaving the last thirty miles for a further recce when we had built the road this far. We now had ninety miles of country ready to be turned into a road, and I felt in something of a hurry to begin. That night I checked the stars for a latitude and longitude position to plot this location, before going to sleep with the thought that soon, for the first time in history, the Rawlinson Range would have a graded, bulldozed road leading to it.

Now that everything had reached this stage, with all the planning and expense involved, morning couldn't come quickly enough. Having my wheeltracks to follow, the ninety miles back to camp were done in one day — keeping in mind that a day ends at midnight — and the next morning we were once again on with the job.

"How far now?" seems to be the predominating question on all such projects. In an effort to keep up morale, I never like to give the same answer twice, although sometimes it would be the truth, and this results in using up the supply of miles before we arrive. To cope with this problem, the last four miles quoted, which are closer to twenty, have to last much longer, and the fitter always remarks how the plant sure burnt up some diesel in those last few miles. But by then it doesn't matter anyway.

It had been a relatively good season, leaving miles of dry wild flowers which, like the spinifex husks, constantly got into the machinery and blocked the cooling systems. The radiator on the bulldozer always receives the worst of it and as there are two separate radiators, one for water and the other for oil, the space in between quickly becomes choked. These radiators have to be cleaned almost daily in some areas, and one day during a howling duststorm the temperature gauge registered danger. The work that followed was carried out in one of the most unpleasant "workshops" ever.

Arriving at the turn-around camp the Gunbarrel Party caught their first sight of the Rawlinsons and were all eager to complete this section of the project. The remaining thirty miles had still to be surveyed in detail, and this took longer to do than the previous hundred, There are deep rocky gullies here and water-worn gutters branching out from the ranges, with some of the thickest mulga scrub as a result of the extra watering it receives, and sandy, vertical-walled creek washouts. Some of these washouts are about as wide as a Land-Rover and as deep. Trying to cross one at a likely spot the vehicle became embedded and, after much churning in the space allotted me, I managed to turn in a way that would allow it to be driven backwards or forward along the dry creek bed, with no hope of being able to return to either bank. Ruefully thinking of the large bulldozer only twenty miles away, I took a geological hammer from the tool box and began digging at the bank, having first manoeuvred the vehicle against one side of the miniature canyon in order to be able to open the door. Accomplishing in hours what several days later took only minutes with the dozer, I slowly made a ramp and was free at last.

Officially we'd had four miles to go for the past week, but at last I could begin the count down again as the flat-topped rise of our immediate destination came into sight, with the great slopes and rocky cliffs of the Rawlinsons in the very close background.

As we bulldozed our way up the remaining slope, on top of which were the three now not-so-lonely stones, I jokingly asked the fitter where he thought we were. He pleaded in a tired voice, "Don't ask me, mate. I don't even know what State we're in."

A signal was sent to headquarters that the road to the Giles site was through, and that the semi-trailers, which had been loaded and were waiting, could start coming.

During dinner that day, the cook had decided to do some washing which he had hung out to dry on a rope line slung around a tree and attached to the ration truck. Everyone was hurrying to get to the site and nobody noticed our fire creeping towards the truck. Disaster was averted when the handyman beat it out, but not before the clothes-line snapped, dropping all the cook's clothes into the fire. He arrived at the site with only what he stood up in, creating a record for travelling light to Giles.

Staring at the three stones, which marked the reason for all our work, Grader Garbo said something about who else in the world would make four hundred miles of road to this. A great deal had to be done by our party before we could think of continuing the project, but there was a genial air of satisfaction at the successful completion of this stage in the work. This feeling always comes after the relaxing of long periods of routine, especially when the result of our efforts can be seen by all who had a hand in obtaining it.

The forked tree hydraulic press brought back some memories. It had taken weeks to make the trip from the airfield, and months to make the road, and now the same trip could be done in hours. Visions of bent copper wire and heat that humans weren't meant to endure came to me as I sat in the same dry creek bed that had served as the water pump workshop. The hole that Mr Expedition had dug for water was now dust dry, and I realized how lucky we had been when later on the bulldozer tried unsuccessfully to find water. The huge machine, with its noise and power invading the peace and quiet of the ranges, seemed strangely out of place. For the first time I had some misgivings about being involved — a fleeting insight into the feelings the aboriginals must have had when they saw the first white settlers arriving in ships they were powerless to stop, trespassing on waters that had been theirs for centuries.

Projects such as this, however, must keep abreast of progress, and many share in the ultimate benefits. Even the aboriginals, as in a case when a flying doctor plane, on a mercy trip to a member of a tribe, flew around instead of through a storm, which was located and radioed through by the Giles Meteorological Station.

8

The Birth of an Outpost

Earlier arrangements, made with a view to the water supply
for the site, had now to be finalized without delay; water is
always the first consideration in the establishment of a new
settlement of any kind. We hoped that a supply was under-
ground, and a boring plant was already being railed to our
nearest siding, five hundred miles away, as the bore sites
were being chosen with an eye to topography and geological
formations. The grader was our only means of towing such
a heavy trailer as a water-boring plant over our new and
"heavy" uncompacted road, so it was now necessary to
prepare it for the thousand-mile return trip.

We had noticed smoke from the aboriginals' fires coming
closer each day, and knew that soon actual contact with our
camp would be made — our presence in the area had certainly been general knowledge with the tribe for many days.
The noise of our machinery would have announced our
arrival to them long before we had come within sight of the
end of this section of the road, and it was difficult to imagine
what they must have thought about it all. Never before had
a massive bulldozer invaded their country, and we wondered if their campfire conversations were ones of fear, awe,
or indifferent acceptance of the inevitable.

One cold windy morning, as we were preparing the
grader and carrying out the much-needed mechanical maintenance for the trip back to the railhead, an old bearded
aboriginal, alone and completely naked, came into sight a

hundred yards away through the mulga trees, and slowly
approached our camp with his head lowered. Without looking up he stopped about forty yards short of us, laid down
his spears, and, with the aid of a smouldering fire-stick
which he carried, made a small blaze of saltbush roots and
sticks, and stood waiting. The dozer driver and I walked
over equally slowly to meet him. When we were within
fifteen yards he seemed to make up his mind about something and suddenly grabbed for the ground. We hesitated
in our tracks, ready to dodge a possible spear, but he only
added some more sticks to his fire. Breathing easier, we
went on and stood opposite him, our hands outstretched to
the warmth. His eyes were still lowered; not one word had
been spoken. After a minute or so of silence, I tried several
words of the only native language I knew to see if he understood. Asking him if he had any others with him, and if so
would he invite them along, we were astounded at the sudden reaction. He launched into a speech, at machine-gun
speed, which lasted at least ten minutes, apparently
assuming that we knew his kind of talk. We stood there
helpless, understanding only about one word every three
minutes, and then he stopped abruptly, turned around, and
lifted his hand. Seven more aboriginals immediately
materialized out of the mulga, noiselessly glided over to join
us, and sat down naked on the ground, in a semicircle
around the little smoky fire — and waited. The group
included several women and children, and appeared to be
two families; they had with them some perfect skeletons of
their pet dingo dogs. I had found from previous experience
that one sure way to relax the atmosphere, in a situation
such as this, was to draw a cartoon picture of one of them,
or one of their dogs. So I sketched one of their dogs sitting
in front of the fire, complete with ribs, and handed it over
for their inspection. The effect was immediate, and within
seconds all barriers had fallen away with the group chat-
tering and laughingly pointing to the dog.

At this stage in the proceedings, our cook came over with
a few pieces of of tinned meat and some damper on a lid
from a cardboard carton, and put it on the ground in front
of them. They didn't even look at it. The bearded man, who

seemed to be their chief, was still talking faster than ever, and after five minutes had gone by we began to wonder if they were ever going to take the food. Then the chief stopped talking, moved around the fire, and slowly bent down to take a piece of meat. There was still no movement from the others until he placed it in his mouth. A mad scramble followed, leaving the cardboard bare except for a little fat, which the leader picked up and smeared over his body and face. This gave him a degree of insulation against the bitterly cold wind that was still blowing.

They eventually walked back into the bush and we went on with our preparations, knowing we would be seeing more of our new friends in the future.

Leaving the cook and dozer driver in charge of the camp we were soon under way back along our new road, with a truck for supplies of fuel for the grader, which set the slow pace in front, and a Land-Rover, to collect the boring plant we hoped would be the means of supplying the new site with water.

The Happy Family were eager to hear how everthing had gone and what sort of country was "out there'. We lumbered into their station after a dusty drive lasting half a week. The truck had used a gallon of fuel for every mile or two travelled, but with no other trouble to deal with we could put up with that and were able to push on next morning after a pleasent evening of lively talking. The next night we were at the homestead of our starting point, and were now on the old-established last hundred miles of hard bush road to the rail siding.

When we arrived we were pleased to see the big boring plant already there and we went over to check the incidental equipment that always goes with it. The enormous spanners and the forge for heating and sharpening the six-inch diameter bits were there, along with many bags of coke, spare cable, and heavy iron sinker bars, but there didn't seem to be any bore-casing, which is most important to line the drilled holes. It is made up of a number of lengths of tubing, in this case six inches in diameter, and threaded at both ends for joining together, as when it is inserted in the ground its job is to hold the earth back from the pump.

There followed a lengthy series of radio and telephone calls along the railway line until somebody remembered the bore-casing had been off-loaded by mistake at a siding seventy miles away. Unless we waited a few weeks, the only way to get it was to fetch it with our own truck. When the complete servicing that is inevitable after a trip of any kind in this country had been done, we set off south for the casing while the rest of the party with two operators for the plant began the long, slow towing job west with the grader. We went our separate ways planning to meet along the track to Giles, as the slightly faster truck could easily catch us up with the all-important fuel.

A week later we were all back at the site after not only negotiating the soft road, but managing to survive the envious glances and comments from the station people as they literally drooled over our prize possession. Water-finding equipment is worth its weight in gold in these dry parts of Central Australia.

Percussion drilling, the name given to the method used here, is something like using a crowbar, but on a much larger scale. The various strata being penetrated, earth, clay, or solid rock, are pounded to powder by an extremely heavy, long bar of solid iron joined to a large hardened steel bit with a conical-type thread, all of which is lifted and allowed to drop by the boring plant. The resulting pulverized material is kept suspended in the water, which is poured into the hole by the operator at the rate of about a gallon a foot, then pumped out as the drilling progresses. Depths to thousands of feet can be reached by this method. Our problem now was to find enough water to start off the first hole, something easier said than done in such a dry region, but this was solved for us in a most unexpected way. Just as we arrived, and resigned ourselves to making a further long trip for water to start the initial drilling operations, black clouds appeared as though working to schedule, and rain fell heavily throughout the night.

We didn't waste any time in rigging camp sheets to direct the water into empty diesel and petrol drums, and by morning we were the proud owners of several hundred gallons of water, ample for us to start on the drilling of the first hole.

The operators soon had the plant in position where work had already been done to select a likely spot. Meanwhile, after making a detailed survey of the terrain round about, I was able to set out a centre line for the station's airfield, and our party began the bulldozing and grading of the runway. In less than a week the airstrip had taken shape, complete with the usual standard approach funnels and crash strips alongside, and only the more tedious job of cherry picking the small sticks and roots from the runway was left.

While I was working on this project the drilling team made the welcome discovery of water, which meant that, irrespective of quality, we now had an unlimited supply on the spot for drilling as many holes as we needed. Actually the first bore produced poor quality water for drinking, but it was good enough for washing and, of course, for use in putting down further holes. It tasted rather bitter, a sign that sulphates, instead of the salty tasting chlorides, were present in solution.

Very much cheered by this progress, and after equipping this first bore with an engine and pump jack, we moved the plant to our second spot. The aboriginals had come in closer and we were firm friends by now; the sight of all this water pouring from an overhead pipe, rigged up from the pump, filled them with wonder. The weather had become fairly hot again, and after much persuasion the native children washed and cooled off under the "shower" until their little black bodies glistened in the sun.

The next attempt to strike water was a failure, due to some extremely hard strata which resisted the constant pounding of the heavy sinker bar and slowed down progress to about only two inches a day. So one morning a few days later we took the plant to a third site at the foot of the ranges within a hundred yards of the spot where stood the forked tree that had been used as a hydraulic press on the Christmas expedition. Leaving the operators to their job, we continued placing markers, made from old tyres cut in half around the tread and painted white, alongside the runway of the airstrip. They looked rather like the upturned water troughs that are often seen in outback pigsties. After half an hour's work the drillers came from the far end of the strip and we drove down to meet them, wondering what had gone wrong in so short a time.

As we drew level with them, they flopped on to the ground as if to go to sleep. They mentioned from under their hat brims that they had struck water already. This had to be seen to be believed, so we all hurried down to the plant, where, sure enough, at a depth of seven feet water could be seen without even the help of a sun flash from a mirror. Although the water was not of a very high quality for drinking, it was a valuable addition to the supply for the construction team already on their way. I was hoping that better water would soon be struck, for our cook's supply was running low, and when the camp grew larger, a much greater quanitity than could be carried in addition to the tons of building material would be needed.

The next try set our minds at rest; at last we had an unlimited supply of good drinking water based on the boring plant pump tests, so without loss of time we moved the engine and pump jack from the first hole to the new one. It is always exciting when, after filling a billy can with the muddy water from the sludge pump and letting is settle, the resulting clear water is tasted. A tentative sip is first taken, with all eyes expectantly watching the expressions of the taster, which indicate more clearly than words whether a successful bore site has been chosen. By the time the volumes of dust on the distant skyline told us that the convoy of semi-trailers and trucks would arrive at any moment, we were thankful to have four good drinking-water bores for them, and two others which could be used for construction purposes.

As the trucks rolled into our camp, we were pleased to be able to introduce the sweat-covered, dusty collection of men to the overhead pipe " shower." The team worked throughout the day and a tent town mushroomed on a part of the rise where it wouldn't interfere later with the construction programme. The natives sat at a distance and watched all this frenzied effort, expressionless and silent until some mishap occurred; then they would laugh uproariously. They made us wonder sometimes which of us led the more sensible existence. One day when we were loading a metal trailer with the aid of the bulldozer in a creek bed, the blade of the huge machine caught the trailer already buried in sand and doubled it up like a banana. The natives were convulsed with laughter and rolled helplessly on the ground until we had roughly straightened it out again. When the same thing happened during the next filling we thought they would injure themselves internally as they screamed with delight at the show.

The construction team were an excellent group, going about their work efficiently, with the usual merciless but good-humoured bantering, and the building foundations quickly took shape behind us as we put in the survey pegs.

They were also in radio communication with their head-quarters at Woomera, ordering supplies and reporting progress, but the weather conditions were not always favourable for a clear reception. One conversation between the foreman and his H.Q. could not have been duplicated on any radio link other than from the Australian outback. I heard it on my mobile transmitter when I was a long way from the site, I recognized the foreman's voice: "Please send a box of screws . . .we don't want any more nails." The reply came back; "I didn't quite catch all of that — I think you want a lot of news and more mail."

"Negative; we need screws, not nails; we have enough nails already to reach from here to Halls Creek."

"Roger, I have it now. You need screws and have nails which reach to Smalls Creek."

"Negative, I didn't get the first part of your reply but it was Halls Creek, H. for hammer."

The H.Q. operator finished the conversation: "Message received and understood. We'll have them up to you on the next truck."

When I returned to Giles, I thanked the foreman for the entertainment, and told him that as the supplies truck had arrived, he must be well off for screws now. He nearly cried as he showed me four new boxes of nails and a hammer.

Top: Offshoot road to a future trig point. *Bottom:* Queer formations make a welcome change.

Several meteorological officers arrived at the camp one
day to begin the weather observations; their information
and results were required at our H.Q. Hydrogen-
generating bottles had to be set up in the open, as the buildings had not yet been completed, and the natives were
bewildered by the huge white balloons ascending daily into
the sky, denoting that the real work for which the station
had been brought into existence had begun. A larger aerial
for the transmitter was erected, and the required infor-

Yaccas are rare in the Centre.

mation began to flow out high over the desert to H.Q.

One morning a group of natives assembled just outside the camp and it was obvious something had happened. One of the women members of the tribe, I discovered, had crushed her toe, by dropping what must have been a sizeable sharp rock on to it, partly severing the toe from her foot. These primitive people had very readily accepted our help in previous incidents involving such things as spear wounds and had responded quickly to treatment. It took only one glance to to realize this wound was several days old and that poisoning had set in. In such cases, especially when dealing with natives, my first course is to contact the Woomera doctor direct by radio, describe the situation and symptoms, inform him what medical equipment there is on hand, and discuss the best way to handle the case. With this in mind I asked the patient to sit down and wait while I brought my Land-Rover along to the scene and raised the portable aerial. The receiving operator brought the doctor to the microphone and we had a long discussion, he told me to amputate what was left of the toe and gave me instructions on post-operative treatment for the patient. I could ask him about post-operative treatment for myself later.

I got out of the Rover to find myself completely alone, with no sign of the group or patient. Informing the doctor that the patient had vanished during our talk and that I would contact him again when and if she could be found, I dismantled the aerial and went in seach of her. The hunt had to be abandoned when no trace could be found, and I was forced to wait and hope they would come again soon, as she was clearly in great pain which would become worse the longer treatment was delayed.

The next afternoon a lone spokesman appeared. After attracting my attention he sat down, indicating that he would like an interview. From the few words I understood and with the help of signs it dawned on me just what had frightened them away. If they had been able to understand the meaning of the word ''amputate'' I would have known before, but as I was quite sure they hadn't ever heard the word, the reason had to be something else.

It seems that not long before, one of their men had limped

into camp with a particularly angry-looking spear wound in his leg that needed expert treatment. So the Royal Flying Doctor Service had been notified and a plane had been sent to pick up the native and take him to hospital in Alice Springs. With much coaxing, and after reassuring the tribe, he had struggled aboard.

The doctor in Alice Springs had carried out an immediate amputation of the leg in a successful bid to save his life, and he was still reclining in the convalescence enclosure, living on the best and most plentiful supply of food and water he'd ever known. But to his tribe's way of thinking, he had been whisked away into the sky for ever, despite all efforts to explain, and they also knew, quite correctly, that the same sort of thing I had used in the form of the radio was responsible. So these suspicious Stone-Age people would rather have a member of their tribe dangerously sick, or even dead, than lose him completely. But now they made a further bid for the woman's relief, keeping the actual patient hidden until we had come to an agreement.

That this sort of thing could be happening in the shadow of a radar tracking antennae in these civilized times was unbelievable; satellites were orbiting the earth, atomic submarines were passing under the polar ice cap, and here were we arguing because of a wireless set. Eventually, the native agreed to fetch the patient, who turned out to be his wife, provided I kept well away from the "wy-lis." He watched carefully as I took the medical kit from the Rover, and as a group of natives, having laid their spears on the ground, gathered around to supervise, I tried hard to explain what was about to happen.

I followed the doctor's advice from the day before, and everything went according to plan. The woman was obviously grateful as she hobbled to her lean-to shelter. I promised to call three times a day with the "lolly pills," and to change the dressing.

During these proceedings several planes had landed on the new strip, and we were able to take particular notice of how the surface reacted. Many aircraft would be using it in the future, relying on it for fuel, and a number of decisions would be based on the general knowledge that a landing field was available. But then there came a timely downpour of rain — three inches in two days, which was unusual for that area — giving the strip a deep soaking several days before a plane was due to arrive. The first thought was to cancel the flight, but as the sun had been so hot previously we decided to see first what degree of drying out would take place. On the afternoon before that landing the runway was tested by driving the grader and trucks over it, and as it seemed to stand up satisfactorily the plane was cleared to make its journey.

The landing was made safely and the plane taxied to a stop at the far end of the strip. As it was turning to taxi back to us it stopped, and we drove down to investigate. The wheel on the inside of the turn had found a softer pocket and had become so deeply embedded that the propellors could not pull the now bogged aeroplane out of it. Using the steel cable from our bulldozer, and much effort with shovels, while the pilots gave their opinion on how they should have brought a seaplane, we eventually got it mobile, the engines restarted, and the taxiing resumed. Our earlier decision, that the strip should have a better surface before taking the plant away on the next section of our road project, was confirmed, and further arrangements already started at H.Q. were speeded up.

Once again the grader and vehicles were made ready for the return trek to the rail to collect the equipment for this new project. This included a water-spraying tanker truck with two thousand-gallon water trailers, a large multi-tyred roller, and a tractor, the method being to rip up the surface of the strip, water it to a thick dough consistency, then roll it solid. Tests made with the red clay-type soil told us how much water to use and how much rolling would give the best effect — it was rather like making pastry.

A few days later we were back at the rail, where everything had arrived, and the return journey was started with all the trailers in tow. The mailman had set off the night before with a huge load of fuel in drums for us, and we wondered how far he would get, with a ten-ton truck and trailer, before becoming bogged by the sudden heavy fall of rain that day. We decided to leave next morning and risk the mud; we had enough equipment to get us out of the trouble we were certain to encounter after the rain, and could also repair the road with the grader after each mishap.

Thirty miles on our way, sure enough, we found the mail-man, sitting on the running board at the side of the truck not completely submerged in mud. His trailer was in a similar plight, and drums were lying everywhere. While we unwound steel cables in readiness for the salvage operation, he sat there with his chin cupped in mudcaked hands, elbows propped on wet muddy knees, and hat pulled down over his eyes. It wasn't until we asked him to try to help with his engine that he told us the differential had been smashed. After trying all night to churn out of the trouble he had heard a loud crack, followed by a most expensive-sounding crunching noise, and then the wheels refused to turn. So it was left to our train of grader, truck, and tractor to free the uncoupled trailer and the truck from the quag-mire and leave them on a hard spot nearby, a task that was finished just as a station truck came along, allowing us to get on our way.

Work was begun on the airstrip the day after we rolled into Giles, a week later. The construction team had almost finished their work. The bulk water tanks were in position, enabling us to draw what we required for the strip as long as we kept the bore engines going night and day, which meant larger fuel tanks for them. As the natives soon learnt how to stop them, and their children found pleasure in stuff-ing leaves and sticks into the petrol filling hole, a nightly check had to be made in order to keep the engines running to have enough water for the next day's work. In rectangles of three hundred yards by ten we alternately ripped, watered, rolled, and graded our way over the mile-long run-way. It was forty yards wide and took almost half a million gallons of water, sprayed at the rate of a thousand gallons a trip, from the bores and storage tanks, and several months of constant work, during which all supplies had to come up by road.

One morning on our way to work we heard the sound of an engine very much like that of an aeroplane, and we hurried along to warn it away. Although the sound became louder nothing could be seen, and when we got to the strip it seemed as if it was coming from the machinery. Going over to investigate we found, to our surprise, that the tractor engine was running. The operator was sure he had turned it off the night before, and he had, for the foot marks in the dust all around it indicated that natives have visited it in our absence. They had climbed all over it, pushing and pulling everything moveable, and, as this machine could be started direct on diesel from a battery-operated self starter, they must have stood on the pedal, causing the big motor to burst into life. It was quite entertaining to speculate on how they must have fled in terror when this happened. Luckily there had been ample fuel to keep the engine running until we arrived, otherwise the whole system would have needed "bleeding" for air locks, making a normal restart impossible. When we went to resume spraying, we found that the water truck had also been visited, and the steering wheel, seats, and windscreen had been coated thickly with mud and kangaroo fat, necessitating a big clean-up before we could use it.

When the cook informed us that all the apple pies he had made the day before were missing, I decided to pay a visit to the native camp. The episode with the tractor could be tolerated, and trouble with the truck could be endured, but the loss of the pies was too much. Their dogs, also, not to be left out, had torn open bags of flour and cardboard boxes of other food, having the one really good meal of their lives. The culprits would have to be told that this sort of thing couldn't go on. It seemed that food, to them, belongs to everyone, as does water in a river, and they would ignore other valuable items in the camp in preference to it.

As I approached, they sat wooden-faced on the ground, the picture of innocence, and it soon became apparent that I would get nowhere with this interview. They denied, as wide-eyed as is possible for an aboriginal, all knowledge of the evening's events. I sensed an atmosphere of uneasiness among them, which was explained when I caught sight of a freshly bashed-open meat tin, not completely covered by sand. Making a deliberate ceremony of retrieving the tin,

I put it on the ground in the centre of the group and resumed my place in the circle. We must have all looked as if we had been "too long in the bush" as we sat there staring at the bent tin, no one saying a word, but each knowing what the other was thinking. I began to explain to them as well as I could how they might get hurt if they tampered with the machinery; as it was I had been glad the tractor hadn't been left in gear; and I finished the lecture by taking out a large knife and saying that we were now ready to regain possession of the pies. Our camp was never raided again.

When the last rectangle of the runaway was finished a heavy aeroplane loaded with long-needed stores was given clearance to come on up. We all gathered with confidence on our old spot at the end of the strip to watch the first landing. As usual the natives were the first to hear the sound of the aircraft and tried to point it out to us a good ten minutes before any of us were aware of its approach.

Some members of the construction team who had finished their part of the job were packed and ready to travel south on the plane's return flight. Some of our Gunbarrel Road Construction Party were also to leave on the plane. Our work here was completed and we were ready to continue our original project after returning the earth-compacting equipment to the railhead for consigning, a restocking trip south, and a spell for the party, as by now another Christmas was almost upon us. A lot had taken place since the previous one of the nightmare expedition, and now here was a further outpost from which we could operate during the next year's activities in an attempt to finish our road link from east to west across Central Australia.

We had the feeling as the rest of us drew laboriously away once again on the road south that this time we were leaving behind something much more substantial and useful than three stones, placed one on top of another.

9

An Unshared Nightmare

The country over which our next two hundred miles of road was to cross was completely unknown to me, and the time came all too quickly to begin my recce of it. For the trig survey that was to follow, hills were needed, or high ground at intervals of anything from ten to thirty miles, so for a start it seemed that the road should stay with the Rawlinson Range as long as possible after leaving Giles, before swinging southward to skirt the Gibson Desert.

We had returned to Giles stocked with rations and equipment, including as many spare parts as practicable, and had begun the most important work of servicing the machinery. It was early in the year and the heat was almost unbearable, with the sun beating down from early morning to late evening at temperatures around a hundred and ten degrees. The temperature on the surface of the ground was in the vicinty of a hundred and fifty degrees, not unusual for this time of the year; we wondered how plant and insect life could carry on in that inferno, especially with the complete absence of water for many months at a stretch.

Despite these conditions, however, the survey trip had still to be done, and I repacked my Land-Rover in a way different from that for normal work. Any item that came under the "might come in handy" category was discarded for those in the "will come in handy" one. The big problem was how to carry enough petrol on one vehicle to get through. In this instance the first place where I could expect to get supplies of fuel was a native mission, and I hoped I could borrow some there for my journey back, on the assurance that it would be returned when we had the road through.

With two twelve-gallon oil drums, rolled in an old bed mattress and tied with wire on to the roof, and the thirty-six gallons the two tanks carried, I could travel three hundred miles at the rate of five miles to the gallon; I felt quite safe, as the mission was roughly two hundred miles away. But on thinking it over, I realized I might be forced to make quite substantial deviations around sandhill belts and to hilltops to scan the horizon for distant high ground in order that maximum use could be made of the road by veering near to the crests. The future trig survey stations would be occupying the highest points in the surrounding country and would have to be visited on a number of occasions by the parties who would be following later. So perhaps it would be wise to tie on two more four-gallon tins. Sheer weight was coming into consideration by now and I hadn't got past the fuel supply as yet. The centre of gravity of the vehicle, with all the weight on the specially reinforced roof, had been raised considerably, making it a hazardous operation to drive side-on to a sandhill or rocky outcrop, as is often necessary, without the risk of overturning. But it had to be carried, so up went the extra two tins.

Next came the water supply, a heavy, bulky item requiring a weighty container; I had nothing whatever to lose if I didn't carry it — apart from my life. I had arranged for the water tin, holding sixteen gallons, to be placed in the tray of the Rover alongside the spare fuel tank, padded around on all sides with soft felt. I hoped that this would see me through as the vehicle was already weighted down beyond its normal load with eighty-six gallons of liquid now, including two of oil, as well as the radio transmitter, six spare tubes and two tyres, engine spares and tools, instruments and books for star fixes, and a small swag roll for sleeping. There was still the small matter of food, but in that kind of heat meals hold no attraction at all and only enough for emergencies is carried. A rifle is part of the standard load always, but it is virtually impossible to rely on it for food in this harsh, deserted country, especially in summer. Even over a lengthy period of camping there is little chance of shooting any game, for months go by without a living thing being seen.

A few tins of meat, some flour, jam, and cheese completed the load, and there was nothing left to do but set off. I planned to leave first thing in the morning.

During the night I thought about an expedition I had made in the winter when I had broken a front axle and, owing to the longer detours off course made necessary by the loss of the four-wheel drive feature, had almost run out of petrol. The nature of the sandhills had forced me to stop in the centre of a circle three hundred miles in diameter, surrounded by an area of thick scrub and high sandhills. I remembered how I had lived in that spot for three weeks until a party in three Land-Rovers had answered my radio call for assistance. The first thing I had done, even before making the call, was to observe the stars for a latitude and longitude position to discover exactly where I was, because the battery would not have lasted long with almost no petrol left with which to recharge it. As it was during the winter the water lasted, with care, and my food position was such that when it was eaten, that was that. The operators at the receiving end of the transmission had repeated in detail my position and were fully aware that without outside help I couldn't get out of this predicament.

As the days went on into weeks, I had some misgivings about placing too much reliance on the radio; it was now too late to attempt to walk out, something that is usually most unwise to consider. Then, in the middle of a radio talk as to how their salvage arrangements were progressing, when I was not wanting to appear too eager, the battery died away. This meant leaving it overnight, and attempting to start the engine by hand cranking, and using what little fuel I had left, to try to bring enough life back into the battery to make a further radio contact. Before obliging, the engine waited until my small reserve of strength had diminished and my complete reliance on this transmitter as my only means of survival was brought home very clearly to me.

I had not seen a living thing since setting out nearly a month before, and I was becoming steadily weaker as the last of my few rations disappeared. I had been in the habit of taking short walks hoping to find something to shoot, but there was never anything, except one dingo that could barely get itself away from where I almost trod on it before even noticing it.

By this time I was confined to the small limits of my camp, with the radio in temporary order, but no more petrol left for recharging the battery should it fade again. It was then I was informed that the rescue party was on its way and, with a series of pistol flares fired at night, and after a most difficult trip, the rescuers came into sight over a sandhill. I had heard the sound of their motors and had made up the camp fire so that I could give them a cup of coffee when they got in, provided they supplied the sugar and tinned milk, and of course the coffee. Their first words were, "Excuse us, but do you know of anyone around here who needs help?"

This trip planned for the morning was, I hoped, to be mechanically possible, but I knew the weather would be hopeless. My thoughts turned to another spare tin that could perhaps be added to the already overloaded roof of petrol containers. So, hoping it would not be a case of "the last straw," I got up, filled it, and tied it on. I had cause later to feel pleased with myself for making use of previous experiences.

After an early breakfast I left the camp and headed west towards the Gibson Desert, with the temperatures already showing over a hundred degrees on the maximum and minimum thermometer screwed to the panel in the cabin of my vehicle. The windows were tightly closed as a protection against the flicking dry mulga sticks, but that increased the oven-like atmosphere of the cabin. The duralium roof, by now hot enough to fry an egg, was a persistent reminder of what was to come. After an hour the speedo indicated that I had now covered the great distance of six miles, not unusual in this country, but I felt no joy about it other than being pleased to be actually on my way. Coming to grips with this country and then getting on with the task is, I always find, far better than making decisions and preparations beforehand. Something forgotten could mean disaster for the trip and myself, and lying awake the night before thinking about it is considerably more disturbing than setting out next morning.

There are many small things to occupy one's mind during the early stages of such a trip: after about thirty miles, some petrol can be transferred from the roof to the lower tanks to relieve the weight higher up — a goal to strive for. It may take all day, but it provides a better thought than the several hundred miles to be travelled in these conditions.

Somebody once asked me incredulously how trips like this were possible at all, and weren't the chances of getting through very remote? I had pointed to a quandong tree several hundred yards away and said that it would indeed be unlikely if I couldn't reach it. Once there, I continued, I might have a fair chance of reaching the next one, and simply by not thinking of the distance to some far off destination as a whole, it did seem a little more feasible after all. That approach, I know, has been the means of seeing me through, and helped in some situations that at first appeared to be impossible. You are reminded of the old proverb about constant dripping wearing away a stone.

By noon the heat in the closed cabin registered something well in excess of a hundred and twenty-seven degrees; the instrument gradations ceased at that figure, and the indicator was lying on its side in the glass bulb at the top. All thoughts of food disappeared in favour of the eternal longing for water, but I knew from experience that the longer a drink could be postponed, the better I would be. Then, as the labouring vehicle crawled its way over the hummocks of sand, the familiar feel of the steering wheel pulling to one side told me of my first flat tyre for the trip.

In a great majority of cases it is the near front tyre that runs into trouble and this had happened now — there was a large mulga stake protruding from it. To prevent the stake from penetrating the opposite wall of the tube it is wise to stop immediately, and without even looking I reached for the jack and steel jack plate and began the operation. The jack plate was needed to stop the base of the jack sinking into the sand. The sun was unbearable and the scrub offered no shade at all, but it was almost a relief to be temporarily out of that inferno of a cabin. Although the tools were under the vehicle, they were soon too hot to handle, as the ground temperature was even worse than that inside the cabin.

After one of the spare wheels was in place and the tools were put away, I had to make a big effort to lift the wheel with the flat tyre on it into the vacant rack, for it had been made hot almost to the point of burning by long, slow contact with the fiery sand. Covered in spinifex dust clinging to soaking sweat, and trying to ease the burns from the tyre, I sat on my heels in the small shade cast by the Rover, and thirst finally took over. Sipping the now almost boiling water from a tin mug equally as hot, I thought how much some water from a water bag would be appreciated, but I knew I wouldn't dare use one where water must be conserved.

This was not getting me anywhere, so, reluctantly climbing into the red-hot cabin, I pushed on. The petrol lines alongside the sizzling engine had been left for so long that the fuel began to boil, causing air locks in the system, and no sooner had I set off than the engine faltered, stopped, and refused to restart. The only remedy for this is to wet the lines. I had found by trial and error just where the least water would do the most good, and I sprayed water from my mouth on those parts. It seemed a most unfortunate waste of water, but without this treatment I knew only too well I would stay right where I was. Nursing a reddish burn on my chest caused by an unlucky contact with the mud-guard, I tried the engine. It fired and I was on my way. Grudgingly taking a doctor's advice, I was wearing a hat on this trip, and I think I would have perished there and then without it.

The sun had shone through the windscreen all the afternoon, and as it dipped below the western horizon I decided to stop — a tyre had to be mended, and the day's course had to be plotted on an almost blank map. An astronomical position was not needed as yet, for the Rawlinsons were still in full view to the north, and as I switched off the motor I noted with satisfaction that I had covered forty-five miles.

Usually at the end of such a day, a sort of deflation reaction sets in, and only the thought of the tyre and the plotting made me get out of the cabin instead of falling asleep over the steering wheel.

As I went round to the back of the Rover to get the spare wheel, I saw a movement on the ground among the spinifex, and for the next few seconds I did a square dance with a spinifex snake as it sprang about like an animated length of steel wire. At last it darted off leaving me breathless and shakily fumbling as I unscrewed the catches on the spare wheel. The jobs finished, the call of the camp sheet was stronger than that of food, which I couldn't face anyway, so I lay down on the ground and was soon asleep. To save the petrol that would have been used up by the engine pump, four hundred and fifty pumps by hand had to be put in the tyre and this together with the day's activity made me forget to check if that snake had been accompanied by any of its relatives.

The sun was up about five next morning and with it came the flies, which could never be accused of sleeping in. I poured some precious water into the radiator, after stiffly getting to my feet and rolling the swag in the one action, siphoned what petrol I could into the tanks, and started off once more. The going was almost pleasant at this time of day despite the rough ride and before I knew it I had gone five miles. During the morning I came to the western end of the Rawlinsons and the start of the Gibson Desert, which from a rise appeared to be an area of scrub-covered sandhills, red as far as the eye could see. It was certainly a desolate-looking region shimmering with the heat mirage and I decided to turn south towards some low ranges I could barely make out from my vantage-point. A sea of sandhills was all I had observed to the south from previous rises and it looked as if the going would become more difficult from now on.

As I changed my course towards the hills my thoughts were very much with Gibson who had done the same thing, only he had mistaken these hills for the Rawlinson Range. I was within a radius of perhaps ten miles of where he had ultimately lost his life, and I wondered what remains were

er the years of weathering. There would be a com-
revolver, and the metal parts of a horse's harness
under the sand drifts, but even with the information
the tragedy extracted from Giles's diary they would
possible to find.

as incredibly thirsty and had not been able to eat for
ays, but I did have some water and I knew where I
ing or, to be more precise, knew where I was. Near-
e small rocky range after battling through a belt of
igh sandhills, I found myself in a forest of dead mulga
hrough which I was forced to struggle in order to
the higher ground. From there I wanted to take a brief
f the geological formations and types of rock.

as constantly on the lookout for fossils or any gold that
be lying around, as I climbed with prismatic compass
noculars to the highest point. This was for the most
tant purpose of scanning the horizons to the west and
and of locating further high ground or hills for the
also hoped to discover some relief in the terrain.
I reached the top, I was so dry I couldn't move my
my heart sank as I surveyed the endless sandhills
ga right to the skyline. But a small glimmer of hope
in the form of what looked like open spinifex,
he south-west.

ss not only magnifies the object but also the mir-
is never very certain that what is seen is actually
the scrutiny is done in the late afternoon or
ing when conditions have settled. But this,
seemed too good to be true, did look real, so
a careful compass bearing, I began the climb
the vehicle and a drink of water with renewed

ountry was still a long way off and it would
ort to reach it, but it was a goal I knew would
. After trudging over the last stretch to the
Rover and having a drink of the hot water, I took off my
hobnailed boots and emptied out the stones and sticks that
always collect around my otherwise bare feet. I noticed that
the iron nails in my boots had loosened with the intense heat
and the steel heels had fallen off.

I tried not to see the Rover dismally drooping down on one wheel, but at last I forced myself to replace the flat tyre. It was good that it had gone down while I was away because it'd had time to cool and was now easy to handle; the sooner I set it right, the sooner I could be on my way.

It was almost impossible to keep to the observed bearing because the sandhills were worse than ever, some requiring a dozen attempts before they were negotiated, and others defying crossing altogether. Water had to be sprayed frequently on to the fuel lines due to the added heat caused by these desperate attempts, and the engine often died just when success was in sight. It was becoming almost hopeless, but I couldn't retrace my tracks as on many of the crossings the vehicle had slid down the far side in a small avalanche of sand; and the distant goal of open spinifex kept coming to the rescue.

During one enforced spell I opened the transmitter box and found to my dismay that in the intense heat of the cabin some plastic parts on the instrument panel had withered to half their size and dropped out of their sockets. The packing around other dials had melted, causing the glass covering to drop on to the needles so that they couldn't be tuned, and I began to wonder what havoc would be found behind the instrument panel and if the transmitter could still operate at all. I decided not even to try until it was needed.

I was feeling weak from lack of food, but still unable to eat, and all my actions were now becoming automatic. If only the heat would ease for a while — but the indicator in the thermometer remained in a horizontal position. I was fully aware, however, that this was going to get worse. Another tyre went down that afternoon and, after fixing it with the second spare, the engine began missing to such an extent that it had no power left. This was not surprising, as I had been pushing it to its limit until dark each day. As I was inspecting the coughing and spluttering motor in the gloom, a shower of sparks revealed the cause as the current

Top: An astronomical station for aerial photographs. *Bottom left:* The trig beacon at Mt Beadell. *Centre:* Signpost on the Gunbarrel Highway. *Right:* Another kind of signpost.

shorted along a cracked plug. Pleased that it was such a minor repair, after imagining much worse, I promised myself something to eat that night, but my thirst was one of almost complete dehydration and could not be quenched. I knew if I survived it would take many days for me to return to normal.

Having plotted the position of the supposed spinifex patch, and knowing I was probably well off course in the mountains of sand, I decided to observe the stars and obtain a fresh bearing, so between spells at hand pumping the tyres I set up my theodolite. I couldn't stand up to it for long at a time, but with the observing eventually done, and the tyres away in their racks ready for the next day, I was able to start the calculations involved. Although the speedo indicated I had travelled twenty-five miles that day, the astrofix showed that I had moved only fifteen miles, as the crow flies, from my last night's camp. My first meal since leaving Giles consisted of a small tin of meat and a mug of water, after which I lay down and was again quickly asleep.

Top: The income-tax air raid. *Bottom:* The waterhole that saved my life.

When I opened my eyes next morning I saw without even having to move my head the dismal sight of a tyre that had gradually gone down overnight. I quickly shut out the sight, but when the flies and early sun forced me to get up I found it was not the dream I'd hoped and, after changing it for one mended in between star observations the night before, I resolved to make the most of the early, slightly cooler conditions. A small drink of water served as breakfast.

After filling the radiator, as usual, I began to flog the unfortunate vehicle over sandhill after sandhill, using the new direction. Every few hours, I transferred more fuel from the roof and was beginning to feel quite pleased at having brought the extra tins. The first hint of relief came that afternoon when I noticed traces of ironstone gravel showing through the sand in the depressions; this had meant open spinifex flats so many times in the past that I was now reasonably certain that what I had seen from the rocky range was in fact open country.

Considerably cheered by this, I pressed on as fast as the rough ground would allow, to discover that the country was surely becoming progressively harder. Topping the last rise I saw rolling out in front the gently undulating gravel slopes of the open spinifex. Now, as well as being able to breathe freely, I could, after deciding on one from a plot ascertained by last night's latitude and longitude, at last choose a course I could stay with. It would have taken more than the second flat tyre for the day to dampen my spirits as I looked behind me, in the heat-hazed distance, at the outline of the rocky range from where I had first seen this opening, and at the shimmering jumble of red sandhills separating us. I knew I would never see that range again from a point any closer than where I was. I also knew that this was where the road would be, if I could succeed in getting. myself out in one piece, and that a great deal of detailed survey would have to be done to discover a way to reach here from Giles other than the way I had just traversed.

By the end of the afternoon I had moved thirty-eight miles south, and except for the incessant heat things began to take on a brighter appearance. The open rises were separated in the depressions by narrow belts of the thickest mulga I had ever seen. For centuries the rain had washed the seeds into the valleys, and each succeeding downpour had added nourishment. The result now, as I battered my way through one after the other of these barriers, was a tangled mass of growth that gave the bodywork of the vehicle, even protected as it was, a terrific beating. Before plunging into each one, the following bare rise could be seen over the treetops, but it was always obliterated during the time it took to get through. The undergrowth often became so thick that I was forced to hack a way through, and a flat tyre resulted on an average of every second belt. After about sixty miles the ends of the tyre levers looked as if they had been silver plated, and I thought ruefully of how the bull-dozer would make short work of this later on. Although the temperature was still around a hundred and twenty degrees, the windows had now only to be closed when going through the scrub and this made the cabin a little more bearable.

I got my third flat tyre for the day after coming out of a hundred-yard wall of scrub, far enough away to be unable to return to the shade of a tree and not near enough to the next. This necessitated mending the whole three on a completely barren flat with no protection at all from the blistering sun. I was sure I wouldn't be able to move if I became thirstier. The sips of hot water from the tank barely helped now, but somehow I felt a measure of contentment at being clear of those treacherous sandhills.

All I'd had to eat in three days was a tin of meat, and by nightfall the violent ache across my eyes and a feverish feeling of weakness prevented me from being able to stand up unaided; after pulling up for the night I fell asleep over the steering wheel. When I woke just before midnight, the temperature had dropped to a hundred degrees. I had some cheese and a drink of water, offered grateful thanks that all the tyres had been mended, and fell asleep again, this time on the gravel.

Travelling conditions improved next day, but the radiator was using more water than I could afford, due to the spinifex husks in the core, and I was beginning to have doubts about how long the water would last. I spent a lot of time with the bent copper wire cleaning out the radiator but it was becoming worse. The vehicle was still mobile, however, although two more plug covers had cracked and the fan belt showed deep fissures; but the vapour locks could be dealt with as long as the water lasted.

Turning on the tap that afternoon, I found to my dismay that only a small trickle came out, and soon only a few drops. This happened when the engine was in need of a water cure from a vapour lock and would not start without treatment. I had to jack up the front of the vehicle in order to send what water was left towards the tap, a thing I had often done before by driving the vehicle up a slope. By this means enough came out to cool the pipe. The position was now becoming desperate and I resolved to travel as far as possible after dark with the aid of the stars, a resolution which had soon to be broken after the Rover became entangled in a huge outcrop of rocks, forcing me to camp. It was a very troubled sleep that claimed me that night, and caused me to be up and ready well before dawn next morning.

At first light I found I had run into a region of rocky hills, and as there was no way of by-passing it I was forced to go ahead. The trip had now become an all-out effort to get out alive. I was on the last tank of petrol, with practically no water, and the heat beginning to play tricks. As the vehicle laboured over the boulders towards the water-worn gutters in the folds of the hill, I was increasingly aware of some freshly made marks in the red clay between the rocks that could have been cut by trickling water. At this stage the vehicle was straddling a narrow water-worn gully where one slip would have put one pair of wheels into the gutter for good, so I couldn't relax for a moment.

It was not until I had cleared the worst part that I was able to examine the story written in the ground of a quite recent fall of rain. Determined to follow this evidence to its conclusion, even if it meant going on foot, I managed to persuade the vehicle to clear the last of the rocks and allow me to follow the logical course of the water. It was at the extreme point of a sharp angle, where the creek bed almost doubled back on itself a quarter of a mile further on, that I eventually came upon one of the most valuable finds I had ever made. The evidence of water had been strong, but it was not until I discovered this pool of water, which was several feet in diameter and a few inches deep, that I dared allow myself to grow too elated.

I had been tempted to cut across the sharp corner instead of following the creek bed around, but previous experiences again came to the rescue. I have usually found that water mills about at the bends, cutting a hole for itself, and the sharper the bend, the larger the hole. It was fortunate that I did investigate this bend, for it turned out that there was not another drop of water throughout the length of the watercourse, which ended up by spreading out on to a large flat. I felt sure that some unseen hand had guided me to this place. Stumbling into the rocks in the dead of night, and successfully negotiating that roughest of rocky descents, I had found water.

I wanted very much to photograph the area, but first I went to the pool and, dropping to my knees among the wild dog tracks that surrounded it, drank more than I knew I should in my present state. It was an unlimited supply of the coolest water I'd had in four days of near furnace heat. Only after that long, long drink did I manage to hold a camera still enough for a picture that would recapture this moment. I filled the tank with what I could scoop from the pool before shovelling the hole deeper; then I waited for the enlarged amount of water to settle, and carried on. It took dozens of trips at a couple of pints a time to fill the tank, but while there was water I was determined not to leave until this was done.

The next operation was to top up the almost dry battery, then fill the radiator, wash out that grimy sticky cabin, and have my first wash since pulling out from Giles. Reluctantly I drove away from the miniature oasis, in one way hoping that I would never have to see it again. Making camp early enough to mend the flat tyres of the day and eat another tin of meat, I slept deeply and more contentedly than I had the previous night.

I awoke in a happier frame of mind that worked wonders with the question of the rapidly dwindling fuel supplies, but all the same I decided to carry out a sun observation at

117

midday to check my position and decide on a fresh bearing to my estimated site for the mission. According to my calculations, I was within twenty miles of where I had guessed the mission to be, and as the sandhills were left behind and the going improving all the time I had high hopes of making it — provided it was where I thought it was.

As I drove to the top of a rise, a small mountain range came into view with flat country covered by dense mulga scrub sweeping away to the western horizon. Making now for the foothills of the range as the only possible site for a settlement of any kind, I came upon native footprints, and when I saw wheeltracks I knew this nightmare was over.

Some natives ran out of the bush towards my Rover. I recognized one of them, whom I had seen at the Rawlinson Range, and it was obvious they knew me as they grabbed at familiar objects on the vehicle. It was difficult to know which of us was the more surprised and pleased. Pointing towards the bush, with their lips extended and their eyebrows raised as is their way, they told me where their mission was located. Less than a mile away, it consisted of several stone buildings and a tin shed.

The speedometer showed that my deviations totalled more than a hundred miles, as I had travelled more than three hundred from my camp against the two hundred plotted. I also noted grimly that within sight of my destination I had just six gallons of fuel left.

I shall never forget the yelling natives who gave me an enthusiastic welcome, crowding and jostling for positions so close to the vehicle that it was impossible for me to open the door for quite some time. There were at least a hundred of them, some calling my name, which they had learnt from our friends from the Rawlinsons, and the uproar continued until several white men, with a look of amazement on their faces, pushed their way through the bush.

I managed to get out of the Rover to shake hands with them, answering their anticipated question as to where on this earth I had just come from. I realized that this was going to take some time so I began by telling them that my camp was back in Yulia Country, giving the native name for the Rawlinsons area. My voice was almost a croak to start with, as I hadn't said anything for nearly a week. They made what was to me rather an obvious statement, after I had briefly outlined the route I had taken, that they had never before had any visitors from that direction.

When they noticed my involuntary swaying they were roused out of their immediate surprise and asked me to go in and have a meal before answering questions. Although it was my first meal for several days, I was grateful for the small service held first to give thanks for the guidance that resulted in my ultimate safe arrival, which I concluded with a silent but most sincere Amen.

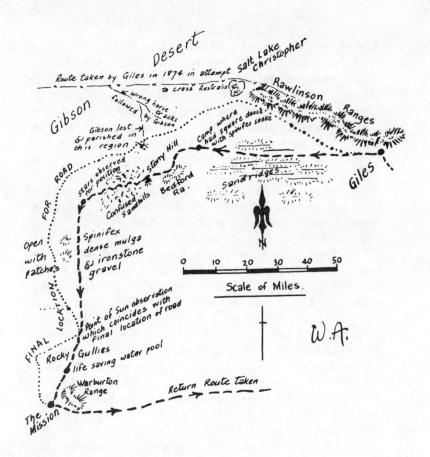

10

A Successful Breakthrough

After three days spent recovering physically, giving "travel talks," and doing vehicle repairs, I was more than ready to rejoin my camp and make a start on the next stage of the project as soon as possible. The missionary, who let me have as much of his meagre supply of petrol and food as he could spare, still couldn't quite realize that the next time we met I would have with me a bulldozer and a grader and that it would soon be possible to travel by road north and east and arrive in Alice Springs. For my part, with my recent trip fresh in my mind, I silently hoped that this would be the case, and as I thought of the enormous amount of detailed survey and hard work which had yet to be done to bring it about, I was even more anxious to be on my way.

The ideal route to return to camp would have been to retrace roughly the one I had just used, ironing out some of the impossible sections and making the third time over easier still. But as the missionary simply didn't have enough petrol to spare I was left without a conscience on the matter, even though I knew neither I nor the vehicle could stand a second beating so soon. Before heading off east to the nearest point on our new road to Giles, a comparatively shorter distance of a hundred and fifty miles travelling in a direction with the sandhills, I went the rounds of the mission thanking and farewelling and promising to return in some months' time, complete with a road.

During the first afternoon away from the mission black

storm clouds gathered, and by nightfall a violent thunder-storm was raging, whipped by gale-force winds. I came to rest with the vehicle bogged to the floorboards in mud. The gloomy mulga scrub, black as pitch, extended into the night beyond the headlights, and I reflected how welcome this would have been five days earlier. I took the axe from its pouch, and by the lights of the Rover began chopping mulga branches; by midnight I had made a wooden road to higher ground. The rain had stopped, so the jacking and shovelling operations could begin. I had adopted a practice that if it were at all possible to have the vehicle mobile before sleeping, then I would work at it regardless of time or meals, as there is nothing more demoralizing than to wake from a sleep of exhaustion and be confronted with trouble. All too often in the past it had taken several days' work to extricate a bogged vehicle, but this time I had it out on hard stony ground before four in the morning, which left the rest of the night for sleeping.

It took one more day to see me through to the new road at a point a hundred miles south of the camp, a distance that took me three hours to cover, instead of three days as in the previous week. The road was still new and "heavy," but it might just as well have been a concrete highway by comparison and I was soon back in my camp at last retelling the story of the reconnaissance for the second time. Everyone was now anxious to get on with the job, and a start was made that very afternoon with the equipment in first-class order.

We planned to make up to ten miles of road before moving camp, which would then be moved daily as usual. But, as if this section of country was defiantly resisting attack to the bitter end, on the eve of our intended camp move three days later the rain streamed down throughout the night, turning the country into a quagmire. No vehicle would be moved for days, and the bulldozer had to be left at the head of the new road ten miles away. After three days the grader driver ventured out with his machine in an effort to repair the damage of the rain washaways. When he had not returned by dark I deflated my tyres and drove out in search of him. About six miles out, the headlights picked up a mud-covered figure trudging towards camp, and I soon learnt that the grader was quite all right on one side, where the ground supported it, but the other half was in three feet of mud. We drove out to it and once again by the light of the headlights I chopped mulga logs, but this time with the help of the grader driver, we had it out on to harder ground in the early hours of the morning. Then we began the slow drive back to camp, both of us using the lights on the Rover. After only a mile, however, the grader was down in an even more hopeless-looking bog, so we drove off in the Rover, never wishing to set eyes on it again. Two miles farther on the Rover became wedged in a fresh washout and required an enormous amount of shovelling to free it; it was a bone-weary pair who eventually arrived back in the camp a few minutes before dawn, vowing not to move again until the country had dried hard. The last thing I remembered before falling asleep was my promise to the missionary — ''complete with a road.''

The day came when we were sure of a successful move. The camp was pulled down, packed on the trucks, and off we went with the good wishes of the men from the weather station. The first truck all but rolled over in a bog on one side of the road less than a mile away. The new driver had allowed the heavy vehicle to drift off the compacted crown of the road into the soft edges, so the following truck winched it back on to the road, the convoy turned around on a small rock outcrop farther on, and we were back at the weather station within an hour. For a country where it never rains, this wasn't doing badly, but actually it was the last we were to see for the next seven months. An enforced spell of two more days was all that was needed to permit us to get away; the wildflowers growing up through the tracks of the bulldozer gave us an indication of how long it was since we had seen it.

During my last trip south I had taken a course of instruction in dentistry, knowing it would be of great help when we were out in the desert. All the equipment necessary had been requisitioned in quadruplicate, and after much study, advice, and instruction, I felt confident of being of some use in an emergency even though I had not, as yet, performed an operation. The problem of toothache had come up many times during our work in the bush, the last case being at the end of the previous year when the sufferer had been forced to make a thousand-mile return trip to have the tooth attended to.

I had not anticipated having to put my knowledge to the test quite so soon. But at our second night's camp, the new cherry picker complained that a toothache which he'd had for several days was now rapidly becoming unbearable; he added that he would do anything for relief. They referred him to me after pointing out that all he would have to do would be to sit down where he was and it would be taken care of on the spot. So here we were, in a situation few dental students would welcome at their first extraction, many hundreds of miles from the moral support of experts who would normally be there.

Opening the newly made, dovetailed, padded, and dust-proofed box of instruments, I made an examination. The tooth, a maxillary cuspid, was far beyond the repairing stage. Reflecting ruefully that it was the longest tooth man has, the root extending higher than the floor of the nose, I consoled myself that it was easier to anaesthetize than its counterpart in the lower jaw. The flies decided the time set for the operation, as their activity lessened towards sundown. Also, in order to have enough light, it was decided to start with the sun just above the horizon. This gave me an opportunity to look over *A Manual of Anaesthesia in General Dentistry*.

Forceps, needle, syringe, cotton-wool, tweezers, and kidney dish were placed in the cook's best saucepan and put on the fire to boil, while the "theatre" was prepared. This consisted of the cherry picker's own bed, with the pillow arranged under his shoulder blades, and an upturned tea chest, covered by a clean cloth, alongside. As the time drew near, the patient grew almost jovial at the prospect of his impending relief, whereas a sort of stage fright crept over me. The water quivered in the steaming saucepan as I carried it over to the table and laid the sterilized instruments in the dish, but there was no turning back now so I loaded the syringe and we were under way. The rest of the camp had disappeared, and as I made the first injection I recalled and concentrated on a similar operation I had witnessed during the training period, and on the skulls I had examined in the museum.

The second injection was made with considerably steadier hands, and we were both filled with restored confidence as it took effect. The sun was dipping into the skyline as I reached for the forceps; it was amazing how loud the noise sounded as they rattled against the tooth before taking hold. Once again, however, intense concentration took over and, to my relief, the offending tooth was soon placed in the kidney dish for further inspection. Permission to "rinse" signified the end of the operation and the sudden reappearance of the rest of the men, who gave the name Tooth Creek to the dry watercourse alongside the camp.

We did not follow the route I had taken on my expedition; I thought that any other course could not be worse. The daily detailed reconnaissance for each successive section became increasingly difficult and the map I had drawn on the first trip proved invaluable for the dozens of decisions that had to be made — such as which side of a sandhill to make for and which way round a rock outcrop would put us in the better position to break through to those open undulating gravel rises. Whenever morale seemed to be at a low ebb these were described to the camp as a cheering goal to keep in mind. I told them of my theory that if the whole distance is broken up into a series of minor lengths, with a point to make for at the end of each, then the ultimate destination seems to arrive at a faster rate. They were entirely unconvinced.

Our work had fallen into a pattern: each day we constructed what had been surveyed the afternoon before, then shifted camp to the head of the road in the mornings, and at the end of the day's work, I carried on alone until dark to find the best course for the next day's construction. The direction was planned using the reconnaissance map and local star observations, taken when needed, and the resulting wheeltracks if satisfactory could be followed back to camp after dark. Sometimes the nature of the country made it possible for me to be back at the dozer and the head of the road before nightfall, but more often than not a single trip was insufficient, and I was forced to bushbash ahead in the dark. In these cases I would try to cut across the lead out tracks on the way back and follow them into camp, but if the headlights failed to show them up in the high spinifex, finding the dozer in the maze of sandhills presented a difficult problem.

To judge from the records, we were now very near where Gibson disappeared; nobody will ever know just how close this graded road actually comes to the tragic spot. From a study of the diaries, I would guess it is a few miles at the most, but it might be only a few yards. Gibson, of course, was the topic of conversation in our camp for several days.

We had all been out in the bush for quite a long time and up to now everyone appeared to be taking it well, until one day when for several disturbing moments it looked as if the isolation had begun to take its toll. The bulldozer driver stopped his machine, climbed down, and declared he would like to have a pair of elephant's feet. When he saw my look of astonishment, he hurried to explain that they were for the bulldozer — which made it worse. It appeared, however, that they were really huge steel discs on a stem, resembling large drawing pins, which fitted under the heavy blade to help keep it sliding on the surface of the sand instead of digging in, and this was the type of country where they would be of use. I was more than a little relieved as I raised the aerial for the radio transmitter and sent off a request signal. The operator at the other end sounded as if he also had his doubts, for he verified a repeat that we wanted only two, instead of four, the number usually sold. When we confirmed the signal, he made a list bid for a check, indicating that the reception was not of the best and that for a minute he thought we had asked for elephant's feet. The items arrived at our nearest railhead, by now more than six hundred miles away, and were collected by our supply driver on his next journey back for the fuel, water, and rations.

One night I returned to camp with a valuable find. The men gathered round as I unwrapped the parcel triumphantly to reveal a handful of ironstone gravel. The significance of this was immediately apparent to everyone — now we were only a day's work away from the undulating gravel rises, and out of these seemingly never-ending sandhills. This knowledge had the effect of a tonic. The fact that there was still an enormous amount of work to be done didn't matter; we had reached another goal. For weeks this had been described as being "any day now" and the next morning the party was eager to get to this almost mythical land. That night we camped on an open spinifex rise; to the south the gently rolling country stretched away as far as the eye could see; to the east was the low stony range that had been Gibson's downfall; we had a bird's-eye view of the dreadful belt of sandhills between. Stark memories flooded back to me of my expedition two months earlier. I thought of how I had risked time and petrol seeking these open spaces, hoping they weren't the result of tricks played on the imagination by the heat haze.

As a rule, a mile of road constructed means only a fraction of that distance as the crow flies, but here for the next sixty miles we leapt ahead, each mile made being a full one gained. In contrast to the previous nightmare of dunes, the small confused belts of sandhills were now taken in our stride and the heavily wooded mulga depressions offered little resistance to the crushing force of the bulldozer blade. Three weeks later, according to star observations, we were within forty miles of the mission. Soon the gravel rises would come to an end and we would be confronted by the region that included the rocky gully with its life-saving pool of water. This area was quite impossible for making a road through, and furthermore it extended across our path, forming an enormous barrier for many miles.

During an afternoon's reconnaissance search for a way round the obstruction, I came out from a small patch of scrub with the unmistakable feeling that I had been there before; I knew I was looking at the bloodwood tree in front of me for the second time. There are millions of trees in this vast country, but there was something about this particular one. I left the vehicle and walked over to it. Sure enough, alongside it were wheeltracks I had made on the expedition, and I knew then that this was the tree under which I had left the Rover while making the sun observation in desperation and concern at the diminishing supply of water and fuel. This was the first time in two hundred miles that I had come across the actual tracks of my unshared nightmare trip and here would be the only spot where those tracks and the final graded road would coincide. As this was quite an event for me, after blazing the tree, I decided to mark it with an aluminium plate, stamped with the latitude and date, and guide the road past it next day. The men were convinced that I knew where we were going after all.

I knew only too well that the old tracks beyond the tree were to be avoided, and it took three days of intense searching before a route around the barrier was found. This involved running the road parallel to this region in a westerly direction and rounding the end ten miles away. Long sand ridges took the place of the rocks, and the road had to pass in between with one side in the rocks and the other cutting into sand. It was easy enough after this spot had been discovered, but many futile attempts had to be made through the scrub to turn the road south towards the mission.

According to my reconnaissance map, and my memory, this was the last main obstruction to be overcome, so this part of the project was almost at an end. There were several smoother stony rises and a large belt of very dense mulga scrub, but these would give no trouble to the team comparable to what they had battled through during the past months. With twenty miles to go we were getting within easy earshot of hunting natives, who would be certain to know of our presence, and because of this we were equally sure that the missionary would be awaiting our arrival.

From time to time we could see the smoke from campfires, and ten miles farther on groups of natives began visiting us to watch the only bulldozer they had ever seen beating its way through the bush. I wondered what could be going through their minds. With no knowledge of compression ignition engines or steel gear trains linking them with transmission powerful enough to uproot trees or brush rocks weighing tons out of the way, how could they explain it? Probably it was the same with all the magic brought to them by the white man — they didn't think about it at all, but just accepted it in the way a child accepts things. They see it happen and that is enough.

Each afternoon as soon as the mission school was out a hundred black children, all shouting wildly, would race around the machine, sending up an earsplitting cheer each time a tree crashed down, knowing that the same task would have taken them days of whittling. One small boy, wanting to show off his bravery, climbed on to the seat of the dozer when the driver was getting a drink of water. Unfortunately, he helped himself into position by grasping the throttle lever which was in its idling position, the action pulled it back to the wide open notch, and the engine burst into life with a tremendous roar. We looked up in time to see a dark, blurred figure in mid-air, legs already running; then it hit the ground, and in an instant disappeared into the bush, with the others in hot pursuit. But they soon returned, and were content to play and roll about in the soft, newly graded dust behind the unpredictable monsters.

Eventually the time came for the construction of the last link joining our road to a second outlet to civilization. There was a mile to go, and in a matter of hours the join, which had been almost constantly in mind since we had left our starting point now six hundred miles away, would be made. Up to now the road had been described in the newspapers as "The Road to Nowhere," a most appropriate name.

The children were in their rock-walled schoolrooms, and the older natives milled about as the bulldozer, with the grader following close behind, both enveloped in a huge cloud of dust, lumbered into the mission. Each operator gently eased on the levers, gradually tapering off the great mound of dirt they had been pushing. By the time they reached the mission road there was none left and the job was over. It wasn't the time or the place to think of the three hundred miles yet to go — a major goal had been reached.

Suddenly the crowd swelled with the addition of the hundred children who had been let out of school to witness this moment in history, and so great was the crush that the operators were forced to stop the machines for fear of injuring them. We wondered if the teachers had anything to do with granting the half holiday or if they had simply been left in the rooms after the students had decided to leave. Now, however, the missionary and teachers were being jostled on the outskirts of the excited mob as they strove to photograph the occasion. How well I recalled my first visit here, coming in through the back door as it were. Now there was a road. It hadn't taken so very long to make, yet a week before it had seemed like ages.

We eventually reached the missionary's house after a shouted invitation to share a billy of tea, and we left the equipment to the tender care of the natives. The missionary and his wife were eager to know all that had happened, and the gathering was an exceptionally merry one. We were to see more of them in the next few days, and we soon returned to camp, each with his own thoughts.

Morale was high that night. Our conversation around the fire was punctuated by the pleasant sound of bedtime hymns, carrying across the calm night air, sung at top pitch by a hundred little voices.

11

The Mission

So far, our two visits to the mission had been somewhat unusual, and only sketchy observations concerning life there had been possible on both occasions. But, during the period following the road join-up, we found that the only true way to discover a place is to live there and be accepted by its people. Our stay was to be extended until a small party travelling out on the new road to our camp arrived. This information had been given to me over the transceiver, and was welcomed by all the members of our camp. The effects of months of hard routine were still very much with us, and a halt was needed.

In the party were to be an officer of the government survey department, which would be using the finished road to carry out the trig survey link; a man from our own headquarters; and a representative from the department of aboriginal affairs. The object of their joining us was to make a united expedition into the remaining three hundred miles of unknown country over which the last stage or our project would pass. In the meantime the rest of my camp would prepare the machinery and restock once again for our final section of work, and as food and fuel were no closer than six hundred miles away by road, they would need all the time available.

Here at the mission there seemed to be constant activity in one way or another. The first night, while talking with

the mission group in their house, and sheltered from the
light rain falling in the pitch black outside, the quiet drum-
ming rhythm on the roof was suddenly punctuated by an
unearthly wailing sound at the door. A loud insistent banging on the galvanised iron window brought us to our feet
immediately and there, mud-spattered and soaking wet, was
a grief-stricken native woman trying between sobs, in a few
broken sentences of her own language, to tell us her
troubles. It appeared, to those who understood, that she had
walked miles through the night to inform the missionary of
the death of her mother, who still lay at her camp in some
far-off, rain-sodden clearing.

The services of a mission girl were enlisted to help pacify
the poor woman and interpret her directions for our proposed journey to her camp, and the mission Land-Rover,
which always had to be kept ready, was brought around.
We intended to bring back the body of her mother to the
bungalow, which was used as a hospital, until the natives
themselves performed their own tribal burial ceremony.
During the journey the vehicle bogged down several times
in the softer mud holes, and we were constantly on the look
out for such traps. The headlights showed us where the
occasional mulgas were growing, so we could avoid them,
the directions being given by a native, sitting on the bonnet
in the rain, pointing. He had been told by the mission girl
which camp to make for; she herself was busy with the
woman in the back of the jolting Rover.

After an hour of churning our way through mud and
water, a small spinifex-covered lean-to appeared in the
vehicle's headlights, and beside it, lying face down on the
ground in the rain, was the figure of the woman for whom
the trip had been made. We gently turned her over on to
a hessian and bush-stick stretcher brought for the job, and
were thinking what a miserable end this was to a human
life, when suddenly we started at the sound of several
moans. The woman was by no means dead, though obviously very sick, so in haste the stretcher carrying her was
placed in the vehicle, protected as much as possible from the
rain with a canvas camp sheet, and the return trip started
immediately.

Any trouble from the bogs on the way back would be taken care of more easily, as we had acquired a few extra passengers in the form of relatives who refused to be left behind. I had spent many years in the bush finding my way from one place to another, but this didn't prevent me from feeling profound admiration and respect for the way these natives guided us back through that wet, black gloom to the mission. Their bushmanship did not need instruments or daylight observations of topographical features.

It was past midnight when the patient was delivered to the nursing sister who lived at the bungalow.

At the first opportunity an emergency call was sent to the Flying Doctor base five hundred miles away, and by morning a plane was already on its way, equipped with a stretcher and carrying a doctor who would decide whether she should be flown out or treated at the mission. Then, to make full use of his visit, a huge list of other minor cases was prepared for him to look at, as actual contacts with this sort of medical help were few and far between. Most of the cases were handled over the air, but the numbers of "outpatients" and casualty visits averaged between fifty and a hundred a day, so the list was quite considerable, even though the majority wanted only sympathy and reassurance. A snow-white salt tablet taken with water worked wonders for a sore knee. An ache in the brains was a little more involved, but aspirin usually helped.

Letters were hurriedly written for the plane to take, and a mail bag from which twenty-five pounds of flour had first to be removed was made up; the sick native who was the cause of it all seemed to become incidental.

Their airport was about seven miles away and we all trekked out to inspect it before the arrival of the plane. It was a length of cleared mulga flat with a dry creek bed at one end, and all stones larger than a man's fist had been thrown to one side. There were no provisions here for an engine failure on take-off or a tyre blowout on landing. A good relations gesture, I thought would be to make a regulation airstrip closer in to the mission for them. After all, we did happen to have a bulldozer and grader with us at the time. Since my first contact with the mission I had been wondering what we could do for them, and this now seemed the most necessary thing.

The wind direction for landing was to come from a canvas sock, which was brought from its storage at the mission for the occasion and was now being attached to a bush wood pole and fencing-wire hook. It was never left out in the weather to decompose gradually — the strip was used so infrequently — and wind socks cost money that could be put to better use. An emu parade of natives made a last-minute clean-up of odd sticks and branches that had blown on to the strip since the last landing, and before long we were informed as usual by the natives, ten minutes before we were aware of it, that the plane was in sight. After one circuit of the field it came in to land, thanks to the previous night's rain without the normal billowing cloud of dust accompanying it, and came to rest just short of the dry creek bed.

The doctor was taken to the mission to see the patient and look into the list, while the pilot emptied cans of petrol through a sieve into the plane's tanks. The flour mail bag was loaded and then the patient. The doctor had decided she should go, and a successful take-off brought the incident to a close. The natives here were less superstitious about planes taking their sick off into the sky than those near Giles, and were confident that the woman would be returned to them just as soon as she was a ''well one.''

Back at the mission we lost no time in making our offer to construct for the natives what they would call a ''nice one aeroflane road,'' and as it was readily accepted we began the survey for the centre line that afternoon. In the wake of the theodolite and line of bush pegs came the bulldozer, with the grader close behind. It was all so very easy with this equipment, and by nightfall most of the area for the mile-long runway had been cleared and had already had its first grade. After another day the crash strips on either side of the main landing field and also the overruns were cleared and both had their first grade; the dozer, which had finished its job, was returned to camp. By the third day the grader had completed its third and final pass over it all, and our job was done.

Dozens of natives were then employed by the missionary to cherry pick by hand all small sticks that might be left, and under direction install the runway markers and wind-sock pole. Only a quarter of a mile trip was necessary to meet future planes instead of a fourteen-mile journey. A grateful pilot had cause to use it within a fortnight. We had gone before that first landing, but we heard the story on our return. A small boy, in his excitement at farewelling the mission supply truck on its bi-monthly trip to civilization, had fallen beneath its wheels, which had passed over his legs, and a plane had been urgently summoned. The strip had been christened. The boy recovered and was returned, and we thought that even if nothing else ever happened, the effort had been worth while.

Throughout the mornings at the hospital there never seemed to be a minute to spare with the endless stream of natives who would appear from nowhere for treatment. It was not important if they had anything wrong or not, just as long as they received treatment. Many really did need the services of the trained sister with their spear fight or accidental wounds, broken arms and toes, and women with their few-days-old, still pink-skinned babies.

One morning when I was acting as intern helping with toothache troubles, an old woman came in and held out her arm for inspection. It was as curved as a boomerang from her elbow to the wrist, and she said it was a little bit sore one after her husband had hit with a stick, and it might-be a broken fella. The sister looked along it as if it were a rifle barrel and told her she was inclined to agree, after which she gave her an injection. When this had taken effect and her upper arm was secured firmly to an iron upright of the old-fashioned bed post, we were called to help to pull the fore-arm in an attempt to have the ends of the broken bones joined before applying the plaster bandage. As the injury had happened the previous day, it now took every ounce of our strength and a long time to make an impression on it.

I couldn't help thinking after my experience on the Giles Christmas expedition that, if it were left as it was, she would have the ideal shaped arms for use in unscrewing vehicle water pumps. When we had finished straightening the limb, and had the plaster in place, all that remained to do was to straighten the bed post.

Ugly spear wounds sustained in fights were frequent, but happily the natives had a rule, which was mostly adhered to, that strikes above the waist line were not allowed. Ankles, calves, and thighs could be and often were perforated with abandon, but this was quite in order. Severe burns were another frequent casualty, often with children who, on the cold winter nights, lay so close to their fires that they rolled on to them in their sleep. The resulting scars are carried for life.

One morning a young man arrived with a series of deep knife gashes on his hands in addition to several spear wounds, one of which had completely penetrated the fleshy part of his ankle. As it was the day before ration day at the galvanised-iron store, the missionary decided to put an end to this sort of fighting by refusing to open for rations until the knife was returned to him. On ration days a percentage of the older natives incapable of hunting would be handed enough food to live on for the week, and the working teams would be paid in money, which was returned immediately for food. If the food were given first they would still expect the money.

This day the missionary sent the word out, but on ration morning the crowd gathered as usual. The store remained locked and the natives knew why, but they paraded around in front muttering and waving spears until it became a battle of wits as to who would give in first. Some started throwing stones on to the roof — one or two at first, and then more until they sounded like hail — but the missionary remained firm. In such cases as this he must not lose the final victory at any cost, but, as he walked about with a stockwhip coiled over his arm for effect, he told us he was glad of our moral support. About mid-day a spokesman approached and said the missionary was wanted outside. The good man went out, and as soon as he was in full view of everyone, he was officially presented with a wicked-looking curved skinning knife with a wooden handle. Immediately, the knife plainly visible in his belt, with a flourish he unlocked the store and the ration hand-out proceeded as if nothing had happened. But the important victory had been secured, and all were silently fully aware of it.

As this incident was being discussed at the hospital, another bush camp boy arrived with the news that a bullock was down the well. Their first inclination was to treat the story with a certain amount of suspicion, for it could have been planned as a final ruse to distract attention while the victory was snatched back by a raid on the unattended rations. While the rest stood guard, a couple of us went down with the boy to verify his story, armed with a mirror for sending sun flashes down the well and wondering if there was ever a dull moment at this place.

There, sure enough, the beam of light revealed the bullock at the bottom of the twenty-foot hole, which was just large enough for it to slip down alongside the windmill pump rods. Luckily the well was almost dry; had it been otherwise the animal might have become wedged beneath the water line, hidden from view, until the water had become polluted beyond use. How the natives discovered it so soon in the blackness of the well was a mystery. It had been able to kick out enough to stand on its legs in the two feet of water there, and even now was straining in a vain attempt to move about.

The problem now was how to extract this great weight from the well, which was one of their water supplies. At first it looked hopeless. Although at the moment the bullock was alive and trying to move about, we could see it could not be removed as it was, and so the first thing to do was to shoot it. The rifle sights were lined up along the sun flash from the mirror, and soon the unfortunate beast was humanely put out of its misery. I had immediately thought of our trucks, which were each fitted with a strong winch, and now it appeared that they were the only pieces of equipment on the mission capable of the great strain of the vertical lift necessary. When a truck was brought it was found that the windmill itself prevented it from being driven to a position where the winch would be clear of the sides of the well; this created some new problems, involving applied mechanics. A system of cross-braced shear legs jutting out from the front of the truck, supporting a pulley block at the apex, was then made from bush logs and attached to the bumper and axle housing with the correct square and diagonal lashings. The weight of the bullock, increased by the superficial friction of it against the sides of the well, was supposed to keep the whole thing down and thus prevent it all from entering the cabin of the truck through the windscreen when the strain was applied. The sideways movement would in theory, according to all the laws of practical geometry, be taken care of with the braced quadrilateral formed by the logs.

At last the contraption was ready to be put to the test. A gathering of primitive natives watched the preparation with quiet tolerance of the white fellows' ways of doing things, and although they had never heard of Euclid or Newton, they agreed that the bullock must come up when the rope bin pull 'im. I was thinking that if anyone wanted a quiet, restful holiday, they should stay away from a native mission. A willing native was given the doubtful honour of being the one to climb down the well and attach the cable to the dead bullock by encircling it around its ribs, a job that involved lying in the water alongside the animal and pushing the cable under with his big toe hooked through the eyelet. He knew that would mean an extra scoopful of flour for him on the next ration day.

The sun was beginning to dip as the truck engine was started, the winch put into gear, and the tension mounted; the rig creaked under the terrific strain, and everyone stood clear in case Euclid failed us. But the heavy animal began to rise, with its sides raking at the walls of the hole, until it arrived at a position where logs could be threaded under it to prevent any possibility of it falling down again when the cable was detached. After the rig was dismantled it was only a matter of dragging the animal clear with a tow rope, making sure not to pull the mill over in doing so, and it was all over as darkness closed in. The missionary, realizing the natives would have the carcass anyway, decided officially to hand it over in public, thus incidentally pouring oil on the troubled waters of the knife incident. The natives moved as a complete community from their camps along the banks of the dry creek to settle in around the body of the bullock, and in less than a day not even a bone was to be seen.

The mission had a small herd of goats which were entrusted to a special old native who never missed an opportunity of pointing to his nose — the natives' method of drawing attention to themselves — and informing us that he was the "nanny goat man".

Another native there had made a foot for himself out of rags and binding to replace the one he used to have before his brother had speared it in the course of a fight many years ago. The foot had apparently become poisoned and infected beyond recovery, and he himself had performed an amputation with a sharp rock.

The replacement took the form of a large cone of rag, twelve inches in diameter at the bottom and tapering off to his knee. It was held in place by strips of binding resembling an inverted top, or plumbob. It must have been effective and secure, for he was reputed to have once walked seventy-five miles in two days, dragging it along as he went. About four times a year he still arrives at the hospital and, demanding the complete privacy of one room, unwraps the whole thing, gives it a retread on the outside and adjusts it all back on again, the procedure taking nearly a day. At the time of the original fight he had retaliated by chewing up tobacco and rubbing the juice into his brother's eyes as he slept; he was left blind for life.

One day at the school the teachers conducted a competition, simultaneously in three classes of different age groups, in which the children were required to draw from memory a picture of either the bulldozer or the grader. We were appointed judges, so afterwards we visited each classroom in turn and examined the finished pictures to decide on the winner in each group, who would then receive a prize of sweets. Knowing full well that these aboriginal children had never before seen such machines we were amazed how much detail they had remembered, and how certain features were common to all drawings. The iron step that enabled the operator to climb up to the cabin of the grader appeared in them all, as did the track rollers supporting the tracks on the bulldozer. It seemed that these items, which answered practical problems in the basic design of the machines, could be adapted to the many little problems the aborigines are confronted with every day.

It showed how their minds work: If someone is high off the ground, then how does he get there? How do those very obvious caterpillar tracks stop from falling down? I know my first observations of a bulldozer certainly did not include those insignificant little track rollers. But here they were in drawing after drawing shown in great detail. There was no

sign of any malice or envy shown by the rest towards the winners; rather the reverse was the case, with everyone as happy for the successful three as they were for themselves, and we learnt a lot about the natives as a result of it all.

Our visit here on this occasion coincided with that of the man who had founded the mission over thirty years earlier. He had led the first party of men and camel wagons from the nearest civilization — still four hundred miles away — and settled here. Now seventy-five years of age, and as active and bright as anyone there, he was accompanied by his wife whose help in the running of the mission had been invaluable. Their son, who would have been over forty years old now, had been run over and killed by a wagon in the bush on one of their early trips. We felt very pleased that the founder should be here in person to see for himself the finish of the bulldozed road leading away in the opposite direction.

For emergencies a few sheep were kept near a second windmill water supply twelve miles from the mission. They had to be constantly shepherded against attack from dingoes by another honoured native and his family, and supplies for them and oil for the mill were periodically taken out. The next visit was due the day after the drawing competition, so we went along also to see the "sheep man."

The mill was in a small thicket alongside a large elongated hole where natural water collects after rain, and when we arrived it was still quite full from the recent heavy downpours. It was completely surrounded by trees and foliage, screening it from view until we were almost upon it, but immediately I had the feeling that I had been there before. Telling myself that could not be the case I tried to forget about it, but it was a feeling too strong to be shaken off. After wading across the waterhole, I walked towards a small rocky outcrop a few hundred yards away and was more sure than ever that I'd seen that also some time before. Then, only a few yards away from it, I saw on the ground a set of faint wheel tracks made by a Land-Rover and knew that they were my own on that first reconnaissance, and that this was where I had come just after discovering the few gallons of water in the life-saving pool. My tracks were within a stone's throw of a half-mile strip of water, and I thought how the trip could have ended in disaster, so close to more water than I'd seen in a year, if that first pool had not been there.

People have perished in the bush in similar circumstances, but this convinced me that I had been meant all along to get through, although I wished I had known this for certain at the time. When we got to the sheep man's camp nearby I asked him if he had heard a motorcar a few months ago from the direction in which I pointed. His face lit up in a broad grin as he sat sleepily on the ground and he told me with as much enthusiasm as he could muster, "Yeah I bin hear 'em, an' I often bin thinkin' after that it might could 'ave bin someone."

We weren't very far from the mission, but I remembered that at that stage in the survey I hadn't any idea how far or in what direction my destination lay.

During our absence the ration truck had returned to the mission and our advice was asked as soon as we drove in, "How long is a towel?" We were a little relieved to hear that not all their happenings are of a violent nature. It appeared that, in reply to their order for a hundred towels, several large rolls of uncut towelling had been sent and would have to be cut up before being issued to the children. A lengthy conference was held during which demonstrations of the operation of drying one's back were given in an effort to decide on the length required. The final figure settled on must have been a bit short; by the time we returned to our camp a hundred and fifty towels were heaped up and they were still cutting them off the rolls.

Anything that happened was an interesting diversion at the mission, and I knew now what an enormous upheaval my first arrival there from the desert must have been in their daily round of events. It seemed as though we had lived there for a long time, so much had happened — making the airstrip, straightening arms, quelling mutineers, tugging bullocks about, and many other incidents — whereas in fact it had been only a little over a week.

Then one night as we listened to the hymn-singing from around our fire, the lights of several vehicles appeared coming along the new road, and we knew that the members of our forthcoming expedition were almost with us at last. We were finding life at the mission very tiring, but we would be taking away many memories. Shortly, one by one, the four vehicles rolled into the camp, and once again I found myself hoping my battered Rover, looking even older and shabbier against these new ones, would last the distance.

It was time to be on our way, but we would be back before long, the next time with a much more complete understanding of what goes on night and day on one of the most isolated aboriginal missions in Australia.

12

The Final Reconnaissance

It was to the north of the mission and to the west of the new road that a prominent knoll had been seen as a likely start for the last preliminary survey as far as our destination. Forty miles back it had looked something less than twenty miles away, meaning that it would be a satisfactory distance from the previous survey station chosen, and although it was probably only a higher spot on a sand ridge it would give the elevation needed to see farther. From a rough plot of the cattle station homestead which was to be our objective, and our present known position on the road, the overall distance to be covered appeared to be about three hundred miles. This meant, as usual, that we would have to be prepared for more like a five-hundred-mile trip, the extra miles taken in diversions round such obstructions as salt lakes and in visiting likely hills or high ground for each successive station in the survey.

The rest of my Gunbarrel camp lost no time in preparing to return to Giles, leaving the bulldozer, grader, and camp equipment right where it was, ready for when we would be able to resume the road construction. A last-minute delay occurred when the cook was speared by a needle-sharp stick from the dry mulga tree on which he had been working chopping wood for the stove. As his axe jarred the brittle trunk, a stick flew off the top and fell vertically, piercing his shoulder, then snapping off and leaving what felt like a sizeable splinter embedded. I quickly put a scalpel and a pair of locking forceps on to boil while the new arrivals carried out final checks on their vehicles and restocked them to capacity with water and petrol from our main supplies. The fire blazed up well with what was left of the stick. In an attempt to ease the concentration of pain at the operative area, and having no other suitable method at hand, we used what I think may never have been tried before as a pain killer. I called it "psychological anaesthesia," as an attempt was made to confuse the patient's mind while the radial incisions were being made from the wood. A piece of skin was caught up in the forceps three inches away from the wound and pressure applied until it became uncomfortable for the patient. Then, while he was using all his concentration on that spot and thinking how painful it felt, the necessary cuts were being made around the splinter and were soon deep enough to admit the beaks of the forceps which could now release the skin and be used to grip the shank of the splinter. It proved to be an effective method, for the cook wasn't aware that the operation was over until we showed him the three-quarter-inch long sliver just extracted.

Meanwhile everything else had been made ready and the little cavalcade of vehicles in the expedition were soon on their way. Plans were made for two of us to forge ahead to the next visible hill or rise, leaving the other three at the previous rise, and for sun flashes to be sent from a heliograph to indicate that each could be seen from the other. Then, when a reply was sent back from the advance pair and compass bearings were read, both groups could move along, the front ones cutting a fresh set of tracks, and the others following in the day-old ones. That each point was clearly to be seen from the ones on either side was, of course, vital to the feasibility of the survey.

In addition to the four Land-Rovers, we had another vehicle of rugged construction with the body work designed and built especially for carrying bulk petrol, food, and

Top: "White ants lower me roof . . ."
". . . but me horses are sound"

144

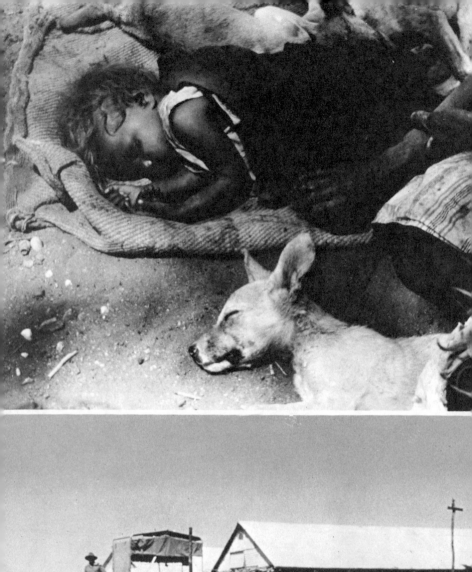

water. It was certainly able to travel over the roughest ground, but the tray with its unusually high and heavy load raised its centre of gravity far beyond what the makers had in mind, and this was to be the cause of much consternation to the driver during the weeks ahead. I had been extremely doubtful when I first saw the type of bar tread tyres it had that they would be any use in this sort of country, but at this stage nothing could be done about them and they had to be used.

We arranged for the officer from our headquarters and the aboriginal affairs man to stay behind with the supply vehicle, while the surveyor from the department that would be establishing and using the stations and I would go in front. Where the proposed point ahead was a definite or obvious hill, both groups could move on together, but we usually found that many days would elapse before the two parties met.

The first knoll was reached in fifteen miles without much trouble, for we were travelling with the sand ridges which ran east to west. But the supply vehicle was already swaying violently over the spinifex clumps off the made road. At this stage the driver thought lightly of it — a slight nuisance only and even a little fun.

Our hill turned out to be just a higher spot on an already formed sand ridge, but it afforded a clear view all around, and we were pleased to see the blue shape of a more substantial outcrop to the west. The rocky outcrops we had skirted earlier in making the road were quite clearly visible and it seemed that we were off to a good start. Prismatic compass bearings were read to every prominent feature and carefully recorded, as well as descriptive notes identifying the land mark. It was planned to carry out the same work at each point, and from time to time positively fix points by latitude and longitude observations to the stars, so that when we noted the vehicle speedometer mileages we could plot our course exactly; this would be invaluable in the subsequent construction of the road.

Top: A three-dog blanket means it's cold. *Bottom:* Warburton Mission, the day of our breakthrough.

The surveyor with whom I travelled was a man I'd known for many years. We were both in the army survey corps during the war, and I had the highest respect for his ability in every field of this work. I had not as yet been camping with him like this, but I knew by repute that he had proved himself capable of being able to live on a rock-bottom minimum of food and water for greatly extended periods, and continue working every night up to hours that would be a physical impossibility to most people after long and vigorous days in the bush. After the last rays of light had gone on the first day out we stopped to camp, made a fire, and rolled out our swags alongside the vehicles. This was all quite normal except that my travelling companion had settled down fifty yards away. He explained that he would be working on a bit and did not want to disturb me.

We had tea together, however, opening small tins and heating them as they were on the fire next to our billy, which was barely a third full of water from our valuable supply. It was a cold time of the year, and we stood by the fire talking over old times, old friends we had both known, and what had become of them, until Bill, as he is known, although it has nothing to do with his initials, decided to start work on the map. I gathered a good bundle of wood and put it by the fire ready to make a quick warm blaze in the morning when we would be very cold; then I lay down in my swag.

I woke during the night and was surprised to see the battery light still burning over at Bill's Rover, so I looked at my watch. It was half past two. It seemed like only a few minutes later that I vaguely heard a quiet voice saying it was getting late. I got up hurriedly, already dressed, and glanced at my watch by the light of the fire, which had obviously been blazing for some time. It was half past four! When I got to the fire I was greeted with cheerful words of approval at my foresight in gathering the heap of wood. Bill said that he had come over to do that very thing when he had finished for the night, only to find it already there, and with that our day began on a pleasant note, as did every one throughout the entire expedition. I was curious about when he had finished working last night, and how much sleep he

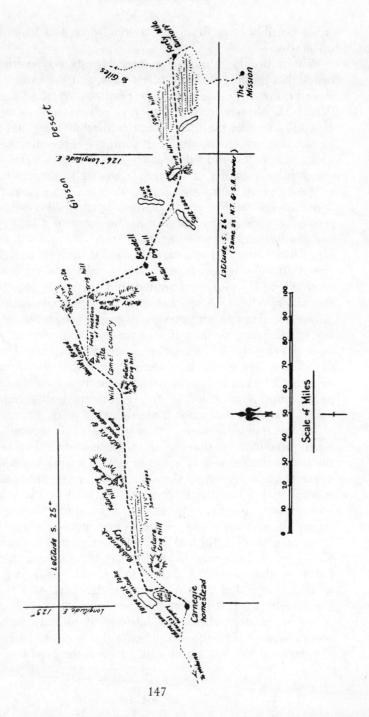

Scale of Miles

could possibly have fitted in between when I last saw him up and now.

Within twenty minutes we were on our way, with the headlights probing into the black bush and the cabin light showing me my vehicle compass readings. We had agreed that I should go in front as my vehicle was designed especially to take the main brunt of the battering and had as well the conveniently built-in compass. The other Rover had a canvas top and sides, which were more vulnerable to the persistent raking of the tree branches in the scrub.

We drove all the morning through many large patches of dense mulga, and as it would have been disheartening to retrace my tracks any distance in the event of a mishap, I constantly checked to see if the other vehicle was still coming. Once, after a particularly hard and difficult stretch of rough rocky washaways over dry creek beds lined with intensely heavy mulgas, I waited, but there was no sign of the other vehicle. After spending an hour checking my Rover for damage and anxiously peering back along the track, I began to wonder if it might not be quicker to walk back to see what had happened instead of driving. I wondered how Bill would be taking it after the few minutes' sleep he'd had in the past two days. Many a man would be near boiling point at having to travel through this country, and it is at such times that a man's true nature is revealed.

To my relief the sound of an engine came through the bush, punctuated at times by the noise of axework, and soon the Rover itself emerged from the wall of scrub. Any apprehension I had regarding the state of its driver disappeared immediately I saw the huge smile even before the vehicle had stopped, then heard the enthusiastic, louder than usual, happy observation, "My word, we're getting along well now, aren't we?" Bill had been chopping off every branch likely to harm his canopy and, as the same ones would be liable to damage those following as well, dragging dry mulga stumps and their roots out of the way. As a result, his vehicle still had its factory-new look.

We decided to check our latitude at midday with an observation to the sun, so Bill sent off a series of flashes to the party at the last point while I took the readings and finished the small calculation involved. He was rewarded by an answering flash, and after the compass bearings were taken and recorded ready for plotting that night and a pre-determined signal sent, we hit the trail, as they say, the only difference being that here was really no trail to hit. We had seen another hill, on the western skyline, which was to be our next goal, and for convenience, although we were in radio communication with each other, we left a written message, indicating our latest intentions, on a stick in between the wheel tracks.

That night, having two flat tyres to mend after tea while the "office" work was going on fifty yards away, I thought that in this case I might be the one doing the disturbing. Before leaving the last camp I noticed Bill had dug a neat hole and buried our two tins, but at noon only my one tin had been buried. The thought that this was very neat and tidy, especially out in this country, put out of my mind temporarily the query about what had become of the other tin. This procedure was never overlooked throughout our trip, and it gave me a further insight into the natural thoroughness of this surveyor, which was not confined only to technical work, and it soon became a pleasure to observe and note the many things he did.

The next day we all decided to meet up for refuelling and compare our separate views on the going in general. No flashing signals had been needed for the last two points as they had both appeared on definite unmistakable hills, so that night we all camped together for the first time since setting out. We were astounded to learn that the supply vehicle had had seven flat tyres already; otherwise everything was going well and radio messages were transmitted to headquarters to that effect. We weren't to see much of each other at this meeting, for Bill and I were off as usual on a new bearing to a high sandhill that would have to serve as the next point.

At this stage we decided that a star latitude and longitude position would be of great help in the compilation of the map, so for once we stopped before it was quite dark in order to set up the instruments. I had mended my flat tyres at midday on this occasion and was lucky enough to see the afternoon out without another puncture, which left me free to concentrate on the stars. Later, with the observations done and the calculated position written on a piece of paper, I started out on the fifty-yard walk to the "drafting office," taking care to leave my light on so that I could find my swag easily when I came back.

I remembered clearly that one member of a party we'd had years before had walked away from his camp, where he had been on his own, carrying a lantern to inspect a trap. It was only fifty yards away, but his fire had died down and the night was as black as it was tonight. When he started to amble back to his blankets, he walked and walked until it struck him that he should have been there by now. He veered to where he thought the camp stood and walked until he knew he must have passed it in the dark, blinded by the lantern. He turned around and walked and continued to walk around until four in the morning when he sat down and laughed at himself until he cried. As he told us later, if anyone had seen him wandering about in the bush all night long, wearing a towel and carrying a lantern, he might not have been with us then, for nobody would have believed his story.

Bill seemed very glad to have my piece of paper with our position on it, and by the fire at tea time we had the usual discussion concerning the country and the survey. It was nearing midnight when we finished, so I hiked home again to my observatory and waiting swag where I lay down and was soon asleep.

The country was surprisingly free of the huge belts of heaped-up sand ridges that we had become used to on the previous leg of the project, and our journey was made over much more open spinifex than I had ever seen before. It was broken here and there by patches of thick mulga scrub, and as we passed through each one, Bill's little axe was often in action and I grew used to waiting at the far side for the never-failing smile and welcome comments about how well we were getting along. Bill had not had one flat tyre, and the canvas top was still unmarked which was a credit to the driver.

On another morning when we had again all met up as a party, I noticed that the supply vehicle and one of the Land-Rovers had changed drivers. Apparently the effect of the high centre of gravity —persistent rolling and pitching over the spinifex — had temporarily got the better of the original operator. We were told he had jumped clear, crouched down behind a clump of scrub so as not to look at the vehicle, and shouted the message into the air that he was "not going to drive that thing another inch." It was understandable considering that in addition he had received over forty flat tyres. By the time they reached us his ill-humour had worn off and the drivers had decided to return to their respective vehicles.

Under one red rocky bluff we decided to use as a survey station we found some small caves, on the walls of which were aboriginal ochre finger painting, consisting of crude circles and zigzag lines, giving us definite proof that this region had once been inhabited. When we climbed the short distance to the summit further proof was to be found. A small rock hole contained about a gallon of water from some recent shower; not unusual in itself, but the aperture of the hole had been "stoppered" against evaporation, and use by animals, with a well-fitting round boulder uncommon to the geological pattern at the top of the hill. This was cerainly remote country, so remote in fact that it was in the Zone A taxation concession area, but nomad natives had known about it first. I was to be told over the radio transmitter long after our expedition was over that this particular hill was in future to bear my name — an honour indeed.

One night, as we stood at our campfire after we had again split into two sections, Bill made the announcement that he was going to bed early. Every so often he felt that he just had to. He also said that we needn't leave in the morning as early as we had been doing and could really sleep in for a change. After this good news we talked about astronomy and I asked what became of the midday tin that was always missing from the hole. Bill showed me a box full of them, each carefully wiped clean with a rag, and explained that they would all be used for marking future survey stations as a guide to his follow-up parties. Made of rust-proof foil, labelled in paint with the serial number of the point, and nailed to a tree alongside the wheeltracks, they shone in the sun, attracted attention, and served as a thoroughly effective and practical sign.

I would not have noticed Bill's meal that night, of baked beans and a dry biscuit, but for one thing: he'd had the same menu every night since we'd been at the mission, and kippersnacks from the foil container at every dinner camp. For a long while, Bill told me, he had solved and simplified his eating arrangements by setting our with a carton of each, and these together with powdered milk, dry biscuits, and a battery-operated razor made his bush life complete.

After helping each other to gather the little heap of wood for the morning it was quite late when we turned back our swags, and I fell asleep thinking that, despite the conditions, this was probably the most pleasant expedition I had ever made. We overslept until such a late hour in the morning that we had to use our headlights for a much shorter time than usual.

The next time the two parties met, much restocking and refuelling had to be done and the supply vehicle was almost completely unloaded. We could help them this time with our supply of patches, for they had run out, having ceased counting the total number of flat tyres after the fifty mark. I reflected that I had surely not been wrong about those bar tread tyres when I had seen them at the mission, but the vehicle itself was negotiating the rough going quite well and was still right there with us, which after all was the main thing.

We were now about two-thirds of the way, and as the miles passed by, my thoughts turned to the large amount of detailed reconnaissance survey that would be needed later when we came to actually making the road. We had been stopped in our tracks at one stage by a belt of salt lakes and were forced to slide the vehicles down hills made entirely of gypsum, the white powdery substance from which plaster of Paris is made. That was one place where the road would have to take a substantial detour. One saving feature was that the usual battle with the sandhills was so far at a minimum.

Our remaining bread supply, which we kept in plastic containers, was found to be bright green mould to the centre of each loaf and had to be thrown away. This must have secretly strengthened Bill's faith in his dry biscuits, which of course were still as good as ever. The aboriginal affairs member of the party that night made the best damper of his career; we all camped together, and everyone had a share of the fresh "survey cake" — a name we gave to anything fashioned from flour in the bush.

Another astrofix that night checked our exact position, progress was plotted on the recce map fifty yards away, and we were ready to move off again in the early morning armed with a new bearing.

Several days later we found ourselves on the banks of an enormous salt lake, so vast that it disappeared into an unbroken skyline. We knew that this lay to the north of our destination, so if we skirted the lake around its south-eastern shore, we must soon cut some defined station tracks that would lead back to the homestead. Our trip was quickly and successfully drawing to a close. We all looked very dirty and disreputable, so we camped at daylight in order to find our clean shirts and rub a wet cloth over ourselves. This was using the water recklessly, as the most we could have expected throughout the previous weeks was a *moist* cloth. Since striking a station track we had been able to drive well over five miles an hour, and in back-wheel drive only, so we felt in high spirits as we unrolled our swags. That is, all except the supply vehicle's driver, who had been worried for some time with an ever increasing, nagging toothache. It had become so bad that he said perhaps I could have a look at it after all when we arrived at the homestead.

A few miles farther, and the familiar sight of the flying doctor wireless aerials rising above the level of the mulga scrub gave us our first glimpse of civilization and an indication of the actual whereabouts of the homestead. It was, as always in these circumstances, a relief after the weeks of bushbashing to be safely through to our destination and not broken down miserably somewhere, needing much wasted work of salvaging.

It all had to be done again to make the road, but that was

looking into the future and could not depress our spirits yet. This remote cattle station was at least connected to the settled areas lying to the west of it by roads of the inhabitants' own making. Thoughts such as these were occupying my mind as we drove up to the homestead and nonchalantly asked the slightly amazed lady of the house whether it would be all right if we could use her stove to boil up some forceps.

They already had word of our intended trip, as fresh supplies of fuel had been sent to their station by mail truck to wait for us. During the survey the supply truck must have had almost seventy flat tyres; the rest of us averaged about half a dozen or so each, with the exception of Bill, who thanks to his little axe made the whole trip without any. The cattleman rode up before long, and soon we were sitting in the comfort of their lounge room, looking as out of place there as bulls in a china shop.

Over mugs of tea and plates of survey cakes we embarked on another travel talk, answering to the best of our ability questions about how much good feed there was and how much stock you could expect to be able to run "out there." At the same time I was busy trying to protect their floors from being gouged by the sharp edge of the replaced steel heels of my hobnailed boots. To keep them flat on the coverings proved an almost anatomical impossibility from my position on the low comfortable lounge chair, so, screened from view by the coffee table, I took them off.

Central Australia had now been crossed from east to west for the first time by motor vehicle. But any sense of achievement or natural satisfaction that usually accompanies moments such as these is pushed into the back of our minds at the time, for there are more practical things demanding attention.

13

A Lull Before the Last Lunge

As soon as the initial flood of questions had been answered and our news had been given, the cattleman began to relate a long sad story to us. Out at his native stockboy's camp, two of the women had been suffering with acute toothache for a fortnight, and they had delayed going for help for as long as possible, as the return trip involved about seven hundred miles of travelling. It slowly became obvious that the sight of the array of gleaming dental instruments on the kitchen table had given him ideas.

As if the thought had just come to us, we suggested that perhaps we could help them is some way, whereupon, as if the thought had just struck him, he said yes, maybe we could. I had been putting on my boots again while he was talking; I saw the way the conversation was tending, and now we climbed up from our chairs and I followed him out to his station truck, collecting the "little white box" from the kitchen on the way.

The camp was near by, on the only existing station road access to anywhere, and we reached there inside ten minutes, eight of which were used up in opening and shutting gates. The natives were visibly surprised to see me and couldn't understand where I had come from, for they knew that no one had arrived at the station along their one and only main road that morning, or even, as we found out later, for the previous fortnight. The cattleman proceeded to explain. "This white fella just bin come from the

Rubberneck country so's he can fix 'em up sore tooth,'' which statement only served to make them laugh in disbelief as they carefully pointed out that no white fella ever bin come from the Rubberneck country. For all that, there seemed to be an element of doubt in their tone; for where else indeed could we have come from?

Sitting apart from the others in the two-inch-thick dust on the ground alongside a hessian lean-to were the two patients, each holding a rag to her mouth and rocking slowly back and forth. Their eyes were downcast and as they moved low moans which periodically increased in intensity were to be heard. We went over and, after I was introduced, I made a quick examination of the teeth that were giving trouble. Without further waste of time the appropriate forceps and instruments were in a billy of water on their fire to boil. Two of the teeth pointed out had been worn down below the gum line by constantly eating meat impregnated with sand and dust, and each now appeared as a small white disc in the bottom of a depression surrounded by pink flesh. The other two that had been indicated by a gnarled black finger had each been broken half away, leaving a sharp point with a vertical razor edge, and they were already loose. While waiting for instruments to be sterilized, I decided to satisfy my curiousity about this "Rubberneck country."

It seemed that many years ago the station had erected a stock tank and windmill several miles to the east of the homestead and enlisted the aid of an old blackfellow to keep an eye on the supply of water in it. This old native had come in from somewhere farther east again where no man's land, or rather no white man's land, began, and after much explanation and advice from the station blacks he finally understood what was wanted of him in return for a regular supply of "blour, dee, and shooga." He simply had to let the station know if ever the tank became empty.

The cattleman, on his first routine ration visit, found the native, partly hidden from view, standing at the side of the six-foot-high tank with his head over the rim surveying the level of the water. Assuming him to be standing on a stump or log, the man left his truck and walked around to him,

only to be amazed to see his toes still on the ground and his neck seemingly stretched to twice its length and arched, so that his head was above the edge of the tank and he could look inside. Now that he had company, the native retracted his neck, permitting his head to return to its normal position on his shoulders, and in doing so acquired the name of Rubberneck. He had since passed away, but the region to the east of the station was still vaguely referred to as "Rubberneck country."

By now the instruments were ready for operating and I looked around for a suitable chair. The best place seemed to be on their own swag rolls on the ground, with a bundle of old clothes placed under their shoulders so that their heads would be far enough back for easy access to their teeth. They both took the injections without a murmur, but inflamed tissue does not readily respond to the deadening effect of anaesthetic, and as I could not talk their language, I was forced to rely on timing and observing their facial expressions to discover when it had done its work. But, as usual with native patients, there was no sign of pain throughout, and the four extractions were soon over. Meanwhile, another patient who also needed help had come to the waiting room lean-to.

After this we returned to the homestead to prepare for the astrofix we intended to observe that night. The position for the homestead had never been accurately calculated, although it appeared on a map; at this time no maps of this part of the country were very reliable. With its position known, we could complete the plot of the route we had taken, which Bill had been drawing throughout the expedition, and I would find it easier later on with the last stages of the direction of the road.

The other members of the expedition planned to carry on along the station roads back to civilization, with a view to returning ultimately to their headquarters, and they had spent the afternoon refuelling and preparing to move off after the evening meal at the homestead to which we had all been invited. Bill was anxious to be fifty yards from everyone to work at finishing the map and making notes for the trip. It happened that this was the night the cattleman and his family had planned to start on a trip to the railhead more than three hundred miles to the south to return a visiting relative. The meal table now would have more people around it at one time than ever before, and in the morning the whole station would be deserted.

After tea I started reading angles on to the stars as the old supply vehicle with its inner tubes composed mainly of patches headed off with the Rover from our headquarters to make camp several miles distant. Bill would be continuing with the geodetic survey reconnaissance, and we arranged that the figures for the latitude and longitude of the homestead would be sent to him after I had finished the calculations. We both knew that this information could come by any one of many different methods, depending on where we both were at the time, so we didn't need to go into the question of how. It could come by means of a direct radio sked arranged through our base station between any two points in Australia, or a note left at a homestead a thousand miles away where he would be sure to be passing later in the year, but he would get it. As he drove away I knew that his little axe would at last be able to have a rest but not so the rustless foil fish containers.

I was faced now with the problem of how to return to my camp near the mission. I could go back along our recce tracks with the idea of trying to cut off some miles here and there to bring the route closer to the plotted distance of three hundred miles, or I could go about nine hundred miles around on the station roads and via the mission supply track. Not considering myself, I felt somehow that the vehicle might not like to return through the bush so soon after beating its way across, taking into account also how it had been punished unmercifully already so far this year. So I decided to leave with the station people that night after the astrofix was finished, for both our directions for the first three hundred miles would now coincide.

At camp that night I was first introduced to the "bungarras." I had been showing the station family some sketches I had made on the trip when one of their small children remarked that I had remembered to include the bungarras. Not wanting to appear ignorant of what they were talking about I said that of course I always showed them in my drawings. Still wondering what they were, I began to work out the star observations, as I thought if I could have them done by the time we arrived at the railhead, I could give the station people a note with the results for Bill in case he was still in the vicinity when they went home.

Next morning some black stockmen called into our camp with some emu eggs to exchange for "shooga," and I was asked to show them the sketches. They immediately burst into uncontrolled shouts of laughter, and then yelled out that the bungarra must be comin' from somewhere else not being like the skinny one fellers they have in their country. They were pleased to learn they came from the other side of the Rubberneck country. Suddenly one of the aborigines pointed to a big lizard in one sketch and remarked that this one bungarra bin laughin', which started them all off again with screams of delight.

I was glad I didn't have to ask what they were all talking about, for now I knew, and told the cattleman that the name for goannas or big lizards they used over here was not normally known in the east. He said it was a native name, and later I found it to be a household word throughout the west. In all the time I had been camping in Central Australia I had never heard the word, and it gave me an idea of just how separate these two parts of Australia were, and how our future road would be the first link up between them.

We called into every homestead on the way to the rail-head and over mugs of tea were shown all the latest acquisitions, which ranged from saddle blankets, new stockwhips, and trucks to knitting machines. Once while having our midday dinner beside a small rounded hill I was told that the hill was empty inside. Someone had found gold in it, and the fossickers had hollowed it out completely, leaving only a shell of rock covered by a layer of dirt. I thought of the surprise it would cause an unsuspecting surveyor if he chose that hill for a trig station and hammered in a peg only to have it disappear from sight and rattle down inside.

After two camps we arrived at the railhead town by which time I had completed the sums and had the position for the homestead at the end of the expedition written on a note for Bill. I showed the cattleman the position of his home on our map in relation to the site already marked on others, and had a job convincing him that he was now in a different

Top: I was the first white they'd met. Their lap-laps, bought with dog scalps, had been traded across hundreds of miles. *Left:* Jack's false foot grew larger with retreads. *Right:* Few Aboriginals are hairy.

place from where he thought he was. He pointed to the homestead shown on his map and said he knew he was there, but I explained that he only thought he was there, for all the time he had lived several miles away. He replied he didn't even have to think about it for he always knew where he was.

I went on to tell him brightly that he need never worry again as he was from now on really the same number of miles in exactly the opposite direction away from where he always thought he had been. He started to look confused at this, so I thought I'd better leave it for him to think out for himself before I became too mixed up myself. I heard much later that he had discussed it with a neighbour two hundred miles away, and told him that a bloke had come out from the Rubberneck country to tell him, as he indicated his homestead on a map, that they weren't all there.

Now it was time to be on our separate ways once more, and after saying goodbye with the hope that the next time we met it would be complete with a through road and the Gunbarrel camp to the new position of his homestead, I hurried off before he had time to upset my reasoning. We had been living on emu-egg omelettes and half a super foot of bullock steak each a meal on the trip down, which was very different from the diet I had to go back to now I was on my own again.

This town was also the railhead for the mission, although it still lay about five hundred miles away, and I arranged with the main store there to cope with any unusual requests they might receive in the future for our project. It would be the nearest source of supply for the next stage of our work and the manager assured me he would give me all the co-operation and assistance he could. Slowly at first, then rapidly, word was spreading throughout the bush towns and stations that a project was going ahead somewhere up in the desert to push a road through from the east. Everyone, however, was completely in the dark about details, I learnt as I progressed.

Top: Giles Meteorological Station. *Bottom:* We never quite ran out of road.

After leaving the railhead town and arriving at a gold-mining ghost town eighty miles away, I was surprised to hear my name being called out from across the dusty street as I climbed out of my vehicle. Somebody had recognized the specially built-up Land-Rover from a photograph in a paper. Then two natives from the mission ran over to say good day. One of them told me that his father was the ''sheep man'' from the mission, the one who had heard the Rover engine as I drew near the end of my lone expedition earlier that year.

The first rain since we began the road from Giles started to fall as I left the ghost town, and it continued throughout the trip that was to bring me back to the mission and eventually to my camp. It was a nightmare of anxious moments all the way as the vehicle ploughed through the mud and slush. Here and there on the higher ground could be seen the wheeltracks made by a small vehicle not more than two days before, preceding me along the track to the mission. When at last I reached the mission, amid enthusastic shouts and crowds of native friends, I found that the tracks were those of a dentist who had come to carry out a series of tests on and research into natives' teeth. He was the first of his profession with whom I'd come in contact since performing my operations in the bush, and that night we spent many hours in what was for me an enlightening talk about dentistry.

The missionary was keen to know all about our expedition and the other whites there gathered at his house to hear about it too. I had travelled 1,500 miles since leaving this place weeks before.

Next morning I set off for Giles, making my first through drive along the new road, as I had been in the scrub in front all the time guiding the bulldozer. Remembering what the same trip had been like earlier in the year, it was a thoroughly enjoyable experience. The programme in mind now was to attempt to reach Adelaide in my own Rover, which I'm sure had taken more punishment this year than any other vehicle in Australia, and have it operated on by our workshops.

As I passed the spot forty miles to the north of the mission where we had started out on the expedition, I saw our wheeltracks leading off the road to the west and tried not to think, at this early stage at least, about how it all had to be done again later. We would be attacking it in smaller stages then, with the help of the bulldozer, and it would be broken up into a series of goals to reach as we went from hill to hill, so perhaps it would not seem so hard. At the same time I knew I was trying to talk myself into something and permitting myself some wishful thinking.

I continued on north along the road until dark and settled down for the night, on the stretcher I had reclaimed from the camp, right across the middle of the road, away from the sea of thorny spinifex on either side. After all, whose road was it? I was reasonably sure there would be no traffic passing during the night. Driving on the soft and as yet uncompacted surface was, as is usual with a new road, heavy going, but the fact remained that it was a means whereby a traveller could arrive at his destination without everlastingly consulting a compass for direction and observing the stars for position. The laborious detailed survey of the best topography for the route had been done for all time.

At Giles I had to tell the story of the expedition for the third time, although the men there had a head start on the others as they had occasionally helped us by acting as a relay radio station, passing on our transmitted messages to the base station. It was many months since I had been here, months when I had camped out in the bush all the while, and this outpost appeared now as an oasis where I could obtain petrol for the old faithful vehicle, some good food, and as much water as I wanted for foolish things such as washing. The next morning I was again ready to be on the road towards Adelaide, still 1,250 miles away.

My first port of call from this direction was of course to be at the Happy Family's station. As I drove I found I was eagerly looking forward to seeing them all again, knowing there would be an enthusiastic audience awaiting news in detail of "out there." That part of the road was becoming harder from the constant rolling by the traffic to and from Giles, and at the end of a day's driving I saw the first of their windmills looming up above the vast expanse of mulga trees. I thought again of their sort of rip-roaring fun, which I'd soon be sharing again. There seemed to be a quieter atmosphere about the place as I pulled up by the house, resisting the temptation to drive right on into the "sittin' room," and I thought perhaps they might be out mustering somewhere.

Just then a blackfellow appeared from his camp near by and hobbled over on legs that had quite clearly been astride many a horse. He was wearing an almost luminous green shirt with bright yellow pockets, a much worn pair of riding boots with their high heels abraded to the same angle as the one his shin bones made with the ground, and a tremendous cowboy-style hat the band of which was composed mainly of geometrically shaped tin trinkets. Little did I realize what a shock I was in for when I asked him where everyone was. He replied in the matter-of-fact and casually unemotional way given to natives that they bin gone away for a while 'cause the man has died now.

I couldn't believe this at first, and he went on to explain that the man had to go to see a doctor fella. I looked at the house, remembering what it had been like on my first visit there, with the heavy motor bike racing through in a cloud of dust, and the guitars playing into the night after the buckets of water had ceased to drench everything in sight. Now no longer would the spinifex-covered roof echo the wild yippies that accompanied each stage of the horseplay, and the sandhills around the house would be quiet at last from the crack of his stockwhip as he chopped pieces out of the damper on the dinner table with it.

Greatly saddened by the news, I drove slowly away to the next station a hundred miles farther on, and the original start of our project, to hear in more detail what had happened. It had been revealed afterwards, to everyone's surprise, that for a long time only the doctors had known for certain that his complaint was beyond their powers of treatment, and that it must eventually terminate his life prematurely. An operation they had performed recently had served to postpone the inevitable end only for a few months.

The little home movie film these station people had taken as we started off on our project had at last been processed and returned by means of the punctual mail driver, and I was shown it projected on the kitchen wall that night. It brought me back to the beginning of it all with a sudden jolt, and I thought of what a lot had happened since then.

Driving south at last along the main road, one that had been made by somebody else for a change, I came on a car stopped beside it with a small girl sitting near by. She told me that something had gone wrong with the car and pointed out her parents, in the distance, returning from a walk for help. Guessing that they had probably not gone the full 150 miles from this spot which would be involved, I went to pick them up and learnt their trouble was only a hole gashed in the car's sump by a stone. They told me I couldn't realize what difficulties they were in now, stranded out here in the desert, so we returned to their car to see what could be done.

After an examination I told them that all it needed was to remove the sump and solder a beaten-out penny over the hole, and that I would be only too pleased to do it for them if they could supply the penny. Noticing the look of suspicion that passed across their faces I hastened to explain that I hadn't had much use for money for some time now, as I got whatever I needed without it. This only made them more suspicious, so I produced the soldering-iron and got to work. When the job was finished I poured into their engine the emergency oil I had been carrying through Central Australia for half a year and they drove off, probably still wondering who would want to carry all this equipment about and no money. It had sounded a good story anyway, I thought, as I looked at my old canvas purse to see if it was really still there.

Several more days passed before my Rover was once again in our workshops in Adelaide, and in the care of the experts who would apply salve to its many wounds in preparation for our next trip into the bush. We hoped it would be the last connected with this stage of the present work, for we were all anxious now to see the first road across the centre of Australia become a reality.

14

All Over Bar the Barbecue

When we reassembled at the camp, where the equipment was standing in readiness with the stores of fuel and rations, we were all glad to be resuming a job that had become of personal interest to each one of us. The attempt to continue the road across the last three hundred miles was up to us.

The machinery was urged into life by the pilot motors, protesting after their enforced rest, and started immediately on the slow trip along the road up to the forty-mile turn off, while the rest of the camp equipment was packed on to the trucks. By the morning of the following day the heavy bulldozer had lumbered its way to our new starting point and manoeuvred itself into position facing west, at right angles to the existing road. Roaring, and with its blade down, it came towards my sun-flashing mirror like a bull in a Spanish arena, leaving the start of the new road behind it. The grader followed in hot pursuit, leaving the trucks and the rest of the equipment waiting on the "old" road until they had something to drive on. We were on the job once again.

As we were fresh after the spell from this familiar routine, the miles seemed to fall behind rapidly and a fortnight later we found ourselves sixty miles on the way. The supply truck had returned to Giles for water, fresh rations, and more fuel, and everything was going well. On machinery maintenance days and in the late afternoons I could go on with the detailed surveys ahead without loss of time during the day; I was greatly helped by the map we had made on the previous expedition.

It was one Wednesday night when the supply truck failed to arrive back at camp as scheduled that something first went wrong. We were not worried when it was not in the next morning or even that night, as it often required that amount of time to clean water from petrol lines or mend several flat tyres. But when two more days of waiting in vain had elapsed, with no radio message from the driver, I loaded my Rover with petrol and set off after tea in search of him. Being prepared for anything up to a three-hundred-mile trip, I was pleasantly surprised to see a pair of head-lights appear in the distance before midnight. He had at least rounded the corner to start after us along the new road, but I soon discovered that the lights were stationary. Drawing nearer I noticed the driver sitting on top of the cabin of his vehicle calmly awaiting my arrival. He had spent nearly four days there looking hopefully in our direction. His radio transmitter was out of order, preventing him from sending a signal telling of his plight. He had enough water and food on his truck to last him for months but, as he said, it just could become monotonous after he had finished reading all the labels on the tins.

The engine, he explained, had refused to move after he heard a violent knock. It was locked solid, with some broken part inside jamming the entire works. He also told me that gradually, as the fresh meat turned bad, he had thrown it well away from his bedroom in the back of the truck. The road was still new and soft, so that towing with the smaller vehicle was out of the question. We loaded my Rover with some of the rations that we were short of in the camp, and I set off once again in the early hours of the morning, having arranged to have the grader back next day to do the towing. The fitter would then diagnose the trouble, and we would be able to send a radio signal to H.Q. for the necessary replacements.

In the morning the camp received the news almost with delight as at last something had happened to break the monotony of routine. Everyone sounded as if they would have been quite disappointed had it been anything less exciting.

The grader was soon on its way back with all the steel tow ropes we had, and the fitter had started planning how to cope with the new problem. He was already convinced, from the description of the trouble, that it would probably mean a whole new engine, and everyone was in high spirits except the cook, who bemoaned the loss of the fresh meat. But there were still plenty of tins.

We carried on with the road construction as though nothing had happened while the grader was away on its mission of mercy, and that night we were all back together in camp once more. Eventually the truck had to be towed for more than a month, while each section of the road received its final grade; the fitter had found the engine to be quite irreparable in the field. One of the component parts was sticking out of the side of the block, making it look very untidy indeed. A message had been sent off at once and other signals were sent back and forth across Australia for a new engine to be sent to us as soon as possible. A local contractor with several trucks was commissioned to collect it from a government depot eight hundred miles away and cart it up to the mission, where we would meet him and transfer the load from one truck to the other. This all sounded most satisfactory, but the contractor's vehicle broke down seven hundred miles from us and he needed time to repair and recruit his other vehicle to finish his part of the job. Meanwhile we just continued making the road and doing our best with what rations we had, towing and using the water sparingly, while awaiting further signals on developments.

About this time the fitter started carrying a huge log on his truck; it hung from the side by wires and rope. We didn't want to appear curious, so it took a month to discover that it was to become the cross member for a bush crane we would have to devise for handling such weights as the broken engine and the new one. He was carrying it until needed, for such logs were rare in this country.

One day we decided to try our hand at mending the radio, which had failed when it was most needed and meant the loss of the fresh food. Using the good set in my Rover, we summoned the expert at H.Q. who had designed this type to be at his microphone and tell us what to do, as radio is still as much a mystery to us as it is to the blackfellows. Choosing a time when reception was best we began the operation by removing the unserviceable radio from its box. The expert had a similar model in front of him and the lengthy step-by-step procedure began. The parts were examined under instruction and replaced; we had told him how we could receive on it but not transmit. Certain valves were replaced from our box of spares, half clockwise turns given to screws and plugs, and connections checked. After each stage, a short conversation was necessary on the other microphone before proceeding.

Hours later, after what must surely have been the most unusual radio repair job ever, the whole thing was put back together and installed in its box. Switches were thrown and, after a warming-up period, word was sent over the good set that all was ready for a test. Nothing happened, of course. We could hear the expert calling in vain, but finally had to answer him on the other unit. We all concluded it was a laboratory job and too complicated to cope with in the field. That same night, however, I dreamt of the solution while I slept.

We had already checked on the tension of the microphone lead connection — it was the first thing the expert had said to do. But what if the soldered knobs inside the coupling had worn down, with the terrific vibration, to a point when they would never meet no matter how tight the collar was screwed? Leaping out of my swag immediately, I looked in the light from a torch, and sure enough there was hardly any solder left at each contact. Heating a soldering iron right then, at three in the morning, I placed a sizeable blob on the two knobs and tried the reaction of a whistle through the microphone on the meter. It jumped nearly an inch.

When the H.Q. should have started work next day we called them up and had quite a conversation with the expert before mentioning that the unserviceable set of the day before was being used. He sounded as if he thought we should come out of the bush for a spell when I told him the answer had come from a dream.

Eventually word came that the replacement engine was due at the mission soon. The fitter untied his log, as his truck was to be used to fetch the engine, while we prepared for the job. We were by now a third of the way across, and were camping almost in what small shade was being cast by my own personal mountain.

A great hole was first dug out with the bulldozer, deep enough to take the complete truck, which was then towed into it. The grader was positioned on one side of the hole, the thousand-gallon water tank trailer on the other, and the log dragged up to lie across each. This was now vertically over the engine to be removed, which was attached to the log by a chain hoist. After everything joining the engine to the truck had been unscrewed, the strain was applied and the engine came free.

Now the bulldozer had to drag the engineless truck up out of the hole, and replace it with the fitter's truck which had arrived in camp with the new unit. The broken engine was lowered on to it and the chain hoist transferred to the new engine, which had been uncrated and was ready. The dozer pulled the vehicle now carrying the useless engine up out of the steep ramp of the hole, and back came the truck without its engine. It was like playing a game of draughts. As usual, something on the replacement was different and did not quite fit, but that was overcome by the use of the oxy-cutting equipment. We could already picture the mechanics at H.Q. wondering, "What butcher last had a go at this?" But we knew they would have done the same had they been with us.

After another period of joining up petrol lines and cables and adjusting the clutch, the finished product was dragged out of the hole by the dozer for what we hoped was the last time. I thought a bulldozer was a necessary extra to any mechanic's kit after this. The engine started once more on the supply truck and off it went for a road test drive. Our camp was again in possession of a third truck complete with a radio transceiver.

There was no time to sit and look at it, however, as it was on its way immediately to Giles for much-needed rations and fuel, taking with it the broken engine to be sent away — as far away from us as the plane that brought the rations could take it.

Things began to settle down as we pushed on with the road once again, and the miles fell behind now that the stores were arriving on time. With the constant moving of the camp, the cook continued his now perfected method of knocking back the dough for the bread with his elbow as he drove, with the basin balanced on a flour bag in the warmth at the rear of the engine in his cabin. It would be ready for placing in the bread tins for its final proving when he arrived at the new camp clearing. Everyone, it seemed, could sense the goal was at last within sight, and their spirits were kept up by the usual bulletins received when they repeatedly asked how far there was to go now.

There was still much hard work to be done negotiating the large salt lake areas and threading through the sandhill patches, but by far the worst part was over. The weather was becoming hotter, and the flies made meal times unpleasant, but these things were overshadowed by thoughts of the final victory now so near at hand. The old expedition map was still invaluable as was obvious from the appearance of one I had been using: it was now in separate squares of paper, having worn away at each fold. But I treated it with as much care as possible, for it contained all the information relating to the exact location of the finished road, with all its deviations and astronomically fixed points, which I had been adding after each day's construction had been done. It was to be used later to transfer the result on to a future publication of a map of that area.

So as the signal pistol flares and mirror flashes were sent, the amazing machinery kept bashing down the scrub, never failing under the watchful eye of the fitter. The plant operators finished each day covered with sweat and red dust, but still they kept on coming. The cook and cherry picker had been having a long, hard, and monotonous job, but they also knew that soon it would all be over. The supply driver and his truck now had a thousand-mile trip for stores, but they kept on with the job. It was here and at times such as these that the members of the party were tried and tested to the limit both physically and mentally, and it proved that the care taken when we had chosen them was indeed warranted.

We eventually reached a point where I decided to drive right on to the homestead to survey the last fifty miles in the one go. We wanted to make the last part look as neat on the ground as it would on the maps, as as we had come more than eight hundred miles, the last link seemed as small as if we were there already. So after observing a star latitude and longitude at the head of the road, and taking into account the one observed at the homestead at the end of recce, I set off on the calculated bearing to make a detour of the last huge salt lake.

As I crossed a small stony tableland within twenty miles of our destination I realized I was in the Rubberneck country again, where I soon cut our expedition wheel-tracks, which would lead to the station roads. Arriving at the homestead I found them all ready to go on a picnic, as it was Sunday, and I had to accompany them to hear all their news and tell them mine. I gathered that a blackfellow needed two teeth out, and that my native women patients were well. The cooling system on their meat house wanted fixing, the piebald mare had thrown another rider, and no rain had fallen. I could only tell them our road across Australia was nearly through, and a bit of a noise was coming from the gearbox of the bulldozer.

On the way to the water-hole that was to be the picnic ground, they had planned to rope and brand a few clean-skins that had been yarded. I was handed a raw-hide lasso and told to try my hand at it from the saddle of a wild-eyed horse complete with bronco gear. This gear is extra equipment for the horse to use to help it in its fight with the struggles of the mickeys after they have been lassoed. My lack of skill meant that I got only one compared to the dozen roped by the aboriginal stockman alongside.

Leaving the station that afternoon to return to my camp for a rest, I followed my wheeltracks made that morning. With a few variations these would lead me back to the head of the road and as it would be well after dark before I could be anywhere near, I would have to follow them carefully. Without them in the dark bush there would be no hope of finding so small a target as the end of the road. It was dark when I reached the stony tableland, where I found the tracks almost completely invisible. This meant walking ahead with a torch in ever increasing arcs, while leaving the headlights switched on at the vehicle. As soon as I discovered where a stone had been moved or a piece of salt bush had been freshly broken off, I would then leave the torch alight on the ground, aim it towards the headlights, and walk back to bring the Rover up to it. Sometimes it would be half a mile before I located the tracks, and this performance was repeated for a distance of some ten miles, until I was once again in the scrub where the tracks showed clearly. It was nearly five o'clock in the morning when I eventually arrived at the camp, with certain symptoms reminding me of my cowboy work in the saddle.

But the day's events for me were not yet over, even though I was ready to drop into my swag. Bending to move a small plywood box from my bed, I became aware in the gloom that there was something on top of it, so I reached quickly for the torch. There, slowly uncoiling itself from its night's sleep, was a snake, which obviously did not like being disturbed at that late, or rather early, hour. It began moving off as I, by now fully awake, watched and gingerly checked the rest of my blankets for any of its relatives. At last I could sleep for what was left of the night.

The route now being clear of sandhills and the reconnaissance finished, we reached the station track without further incident one afternoon as we stopped work. I explained that we had only ten miles to go to the house so we all turned in for the night with a very contented feeling.

But no sooner had we moved off to our swags than we heard the sound of an engine approaching. The astounding thing was that it was coming from the direction of the road that we had just made. We wondered who at this stage could possibly know of the existence of the new road, and as we got up we saw the headlights of two vehicles. They turned out to contain two young men — with a vehicle each — on a holiday trip, who had been told at Giles that we should be almost over to the west with the new road by the time they caught up to us. The news of our progress had been given to Giles by the supply driver on each of his trips. As the young men were well equipped with transceiver and stores, they decided to give the new road a try.

So it was that the first outside users of our new road pulled up at our camp saying they thought they would never catch up with us. They had come almost nine hundred miles. Their engines were running cooler with the night travelling, which explained why they were still mobile at that hour. They had also been taking notice of our aluminium sign plates on the trees and knew according to their speedo readings that they must be near to us during that night. It was an extraordinary coincidence of timing, and after a shower they decided to carry on the ten miles to the homestead in the cool.

There seemed to be never a dull moment lately. Months after this, a magazine was sent to me by post, which contained an article they had written about their trip.

Two days later the bulldozer was within sight of the station buildings, including the warm meat house and the main road leading off to the west and further civilization. We had already arranged just where to come out on to this road for the convenience of all concerned, and the thought crossed my mind that if everything were to break down suddenly we could finish off the road with a shovel.

The station occupants were all out to see the finish as we stopped the dozer with five yards to go, and to photograph what was to us an historic event. Then, with a wild cheer from the natives and cowboys and a sigh of relief from us, the dozer blade closed the gap with the main road, the grader rounded the section off, and the first access road across Central Australia was through. The date was Saturday, 15 November 1958.

The lady of the house was quite pleased to know that she now had neighbours on either side of her at last, but agreed that nine hundred miles was probably a bit too far to go to borrow a cup of sugar. The cattleman began to acquaint the surrounding stations with the news and the invitation to come along over for a barbecue to mark the event. Our machinery was placed in a prearranged spot out of the way, and the native had his teeth extracted. After all, some of the surrounding station people lived only three hundred miles away. We asked whether, as our life was one long barbecue, perhaps we could go inside and have ours on the table.

More than half the return journey to Adelaide, seventeen hundred miles away, was to be back along our own new road, and as once again the year was nearly over we prepared for the trip. Packing what equipment needed renewing, and refuelling the vehicles, we were ready to go the morning after the barbecue, which we had outside anyway, feeling that we had all been "too long in the bush."

It was several years later that the Western Australian surveys teams later brought out their revised maps covering the area of the road and I was shown a finished set of those published. There, sure enough, extending from map to map throughout its length in their State, was our road, with the addition of a name printed along it at intervals. With the approval of the Western Australian Government departments concerned, it was to be named after the party who had endured so much to construct it, and it now appears on maps, to be known for all time as the Gunbarrel Highway.